ROMAN INFANTRY EQUIPMENT

EQUIPMENT

The Later Empire

ROMAN INFANTRY EQUIPMENT

The Later Empire

I.P. Stephenson

TEMPUS

Dedicated to

Susan

And to the memory of my Grandfather

Isaac Lovatt

First published 1999

Published by:
Tempus Publishing Limited
The Mill, Brimscombe Port
Stroud, Gloucestershire, GL5 2QG

Typesetting and origination by Tempus Publishing Ltd.
Printed and bound in Great Britain.

British Library Cataloguing in Publication Data.
A catalogue record for this book is available from the British Library.

ISBN 07524 1410 0

Contents

List of figures

List of plates

Cover illustration: A reconstruction of the Heddernheim helmet

9

Acknowledgements

Many, many, thanks go to my wife Susan for all of her help, support and typing. Many thanks are also due to Miriam Daniels for her superb paintings and drawings, and to Karen Dixon and Richard Underwood for their equally excellent illustrations.

The late Charles Daniels, Lindsay Allason-Jones, Jon Coulston, Mike Bishop, Pat Southern and Heinrich Harke, have been more than helpful and encouraging —many thanks.

Special thanks are also due to my fellow 'Two Ball Lonnen Tetrarchs' Karen Dixon, Richard Underwood and Philip Clark. As well as to Paul Mullis, Alex Croom, and Bill Griffiths, for all of the help and support — thank you.

I also wish to thank Peter Kemmis Betty, Pavel Dolukhanov, Marianna Taymanova, Carol van Driel-Murray, Marcus Daniels, Bridget Anfiteatro-Graham, Maria Miguez, The Arbeia Society, The Museum of the University and the Society of Antiquaries of Newcastle upon Tyne, The English Settlement Society, and the staff of Bulmershe Library the University of Reading.

Finally, I wish to thank my Parents for all of their help, support and encouragement — thank you.

1 Introduction

To-day we have naming of parts. Yesterday
We had daily cleaning, and tomorrow morning
We shall have what to do after firing. But to-day,
Today we have naming of parts.

Henry Reed, *Naming of Parts*. 1946

The history of the Roman Empire divides into four, quite neat, sections. The Julio-Claudian period (27 BC – AD 68), the Second Century which is actually slightly longer than a century, lasting as it does from AD 68 to AD 192, the Third Century which is slightly shorter (AD 192 – AD 284), and the Dominate (AD 284 – AD 476).

The period which is the concern of this book is the third century, which began in AD 192 with the death, or rather assassination, of Commodus and ended in AD 284 with the accession of Diocletion. It was a time of crises and chaos for the Empire; war, both civil and external, was endemic. The Imperial throne itself saw 36 occupants, of whom only four died of natural causes; the rest succumbing to either assassination, suicide or death in battle. The single exception to this being the Emperor Valerian (AD 253 – 60) whom, to the Empire's lasting shame, was captured in battle by the Persians.

The failure, the lack of stability, was political. External events, the coalescing of the German Tribes into larger confederations and the replacement of the Arsacid Parthians by the far more dynamic Sassanid Persian dynasty, merely served to exacerbate the problem. As to the Army's role in all of this, the Army was neither to blame nor was it blameless, for the Army in the Roman World always possessed political potential, it just did not always choose to exercise that potential and in periods of stability did not need to. However, in the political climate of the third century, when the whole world seemed up for the taking (the Praetorian Guard did in fact auction the Empire in AD 193) and when civil war, usurpation, bribery, corruption, and assassination were the order of the day, then the Army's politicking is both understandable and unsurprising. An understanding therefore, of the Army as a political force was a necessity for the would be Emperor in the third century. Septimius Severus both possessed and indeed profited from this understanding; and on his deathbed communicated it to his sons. His advice to 'enrich the soldiers, and despise all the rest' (Dio LXXVII. 15.2) may not be particularly original, but it was eminently practical, and was followed with varying degrees of success by all of the occupants of the Imperial Throne in the third century. However, the masses can be fickle and the Imperial Roman Army was no exception. Incompetence, feebleness and general unsuitability, both perceived and actual, could and did lead to a number of Emperors suffering lack of support; removal, either assassination or suicide, and replacement. However, having said all of that, this is not a history of the Roman Army in the third century, nor is this book overly concerned with the organisation of the Army, which was still in this period divided into the Legions and the Auxilia, although some organisational aspects do, as will be seen, impinge upon this study.

This book then is concerned with the military equipment of the third century, specifically infantry equipment, although a large number of the items described would also have been used by cavalry units of the period. The range of items which can be classed as military equipment is vast, and could include such diverse items as pack animals, nails, forts — the list is endless. This present study, therefore, confines itself to the obvious and is in the main concerned with arms and armour, although standards, clothing and marching equipment are also described. Siege equipment, from the humble but lethal hand-thrown stone, to the far grander siege tower, is omitted, as the subject constitutes a book in its own right. Although, artillery is included as it had a place on the battlefield. The equipment is not however, viewed simply as a set of artifacts, a typology to be listed. Context is vital to understanding, and context not only covers how a thing was used but also who used it. In the third century the 'who' is not as complicated as in earlier centuries, for although the *Constitutio Antoniana* or Edict of Caracalla (AD 212), as it is more popularly known, may have removed any status difference in terms of citizenship between the Legions and the Auxilia, its impact upon equipment use would have been minimal. As by this point there was a marked lack of differentiation between legionary and auxiliary equipment, with the more versatile 'auxiliary style' being preferred by both types. Any differentiation that did exist was based upon whether or not a soldier was classed as an open- or close-order infantryman, and this only affected the type of primary weapon carried, not the title of the unit to which such a soldier belonged, as both the legions and auxilia contained both open- and close-order infantry. The 'how' of use is concerned with effectiveness at both the individual and unit/battlefield levels. The former is dealt with at the end of each individual chapter, whereas the latter is the main covered in the final chapter on tactics.

This picture of the equipment and its use is wherever possible, derived from a range of contemporary evidence, of which the majority is archaeological, but which also includes both written and representational sources. However, such evidence cannot always paint a complete picture, therefore, in order to achieve completeness both comparative and experimental sources have been used. This non-contemporary evidence does not, however, paint a picture of what actually was, but only of what might have been, and this should be borne in mind at all times.

2 Shields

Then coming together in one place they encountered each other.
They dashed together their shields and spears and the force of
men armoured in bronze. Then bossed shield struck against
bossed shield and a great din of fighting ensued. Then arose the
groans and shouts of triumph, of men killing and being killed.
The ground ran with blood.

Homer, *Iliad*, 4

The shield was a portable obstacle, placed by the soldier between himself and danger. It must, however, be remembered at all times that it was the user (the legionary or auxiliary) not the shield, which was the target of the attack. The shield was interjected in order to, at best stop, or at least reduce, the force of the blow. A shield was required because the body armour of the day could not offer complete protection against the weapon systems of the day. The shield was, in theory, designed to give this level of inclusive protection to the body. However, shield design and construction was an exercise in compromise, and these compromises reduced its inclusivity. Theoretically the shield should be large enough to cover the body, thick enough to be impenetrable, and light enough to permit ease of movement. In practice only two of these factors are completely achievable, the third must be compromised. For example, a large shield which covered the body (from shoulder to knee) and which was thick enough to prevent all weapons penetrating, would be so heavy as to be unmanageable. Any increase in manoeuvrability from this state can only be achieved at the expense of either shield size, ie. make the shield smaller and thus lighter; or shield thickness, which would again reduce weight. Both alternatives, either reduced size or thickness, unfortunately reduce the shield's protective capabilities. However, a heavy, unmanageable shield was also a liability as it unnecessarily fatigued the user, reducing his morale and therefore his fighting capability, for in hand-to-hand combat, even in the static shieldwall, shield manoeuvrability was vital, with any inability to block, quickly and efficiently, only proving fatal. In actuality, as will be seen, the Roman Army of the day compromised thickness in order to give the soldier a large manoeuvrable shield.

Despite the fashion for unarmoured representations on gravestones and the lack of monumental propaganda sculpture, the shield is reasonably well represented in the iconographic record. It appeared on a number of gravestones, where it is displayed either to one side of the figure or alternatively held in the left hand, and in both the 'Exodus' and 'Battle of Ebenezer' frescoes in the synagogue at Dura Europos, Syria, as well as on the *phalera* of Aurelius Cervianus.

Taken together this information paints a picture not only of the range of shield shapes used in the third century, but also of their relative frequency. However, the representational evidence tells us very little, if anything about shield decoration. Nor can it tell us anything about shield size. Representations of shields are just representations, they can help to corroborate the archaeological evidence, but they cannot be used on their own. As where they are shown it was merely to show that they were used and it was the user not the artifact which was the important part of the picture.

Three types or shapes of shield appear in the iconographic record; the hexagonal, the rectangular, and the oval. Hexagonal shields only appear in the 'Battle of Ebenezer' fresco, where in contrast to earlier centuries they appear in the hands of infantrymen rather than cavalrymen, although Metope no. XXXIV at Adamklissi, Romania, depicts a legionary fighting with what maybe a hexagonal shield. Rectangular shields appear on only two tombstones, although they also appear in the archaeological record, unlike hexagonal shields which do not. The remaining representations of shields depict the oval type (**colour plates 7 & 8**); they show that it was used equally by both legionary and auxiliary troops, and it was in all probability the most common form of shield used by the Roman Army in this period.

The most complete find of Roman shields from any period comes from Dura Europos, Syria, and dates to the mid-third century. The find consists of no less than 24 complete or fragmentary shield boards, 21 bosses and 6 reinforcing bars.

The best-preserved examples are broad ovals, which measure between 1.07m-1.18m ($3\frac{1}{2}$ - 4ft) in length and 0.92m-0.97m (approximately 3ft) in width (**figs 1 & 2**). There were made up of between 12 and 15 poplar wood planks, 8-12mm ($\frac{1}{3}$ –$\frac{1}{2}$in) thick, which were glued edge to edge. In order to accommodate the hand, two holes were cut in the shield board. The upper hole was semicircular and the lower was trapezoidal. The horizontal wooden grip formed between the two holes was strengthened by an iron reinforcing bar which ran the width of the shield and was held in place by a single rivet at each end. The holes, which ran around the rim were for rawhide or leather edging which would have been sewn on. There is no evidence that the metal edge guttering of earlier centuries was ever used in the third century. One of the shields also had rivets in place for the attachment of a carrying strap, although no such strap was found. These rivets were to the left of the boss, if viewed face on, and next to the upper right rim.

None of the complete examples had shield bosses attached. However the position of the rivet holes on the flanges of surviving bosses show that they would have been fastened to the shield board by four rivets in a north, south, east, west pattern. The

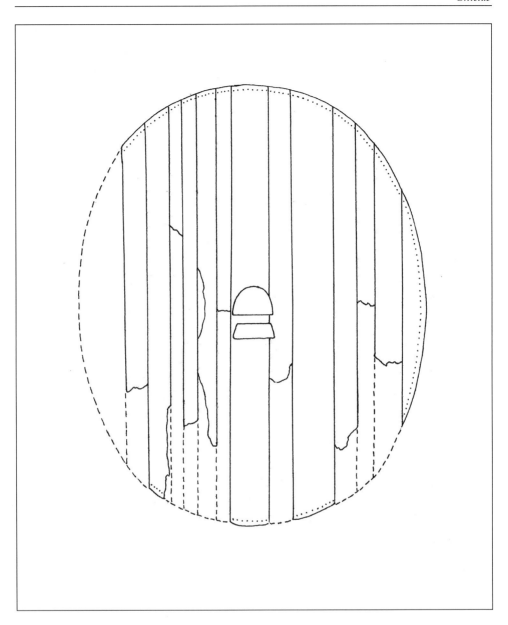

1   *Shield V from Dura Europos, Syria.*

(Redrawn by M. Daniels from Rostovtzeff et al 1939)

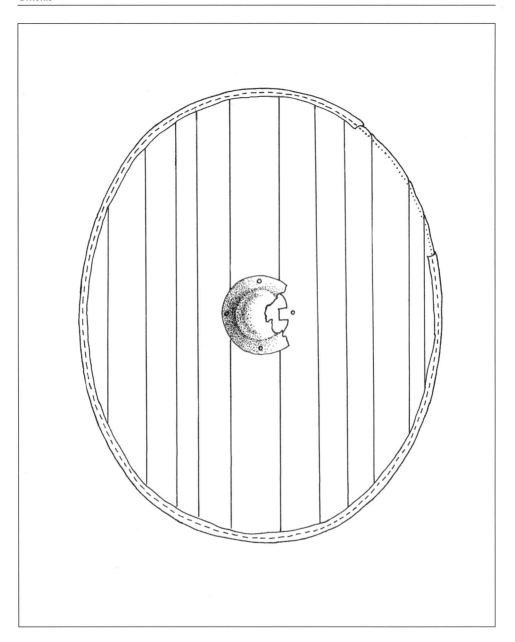

2   A reconstruction of Shield IV from Dura Europos, Syria.

(Redrawn by M. Daniels from Rostovtzeff et al 1939)

bosses themselves were domed and in the main had a flat circular flange (**fig 3**), between 185-220mm ($7\frac{1}{4}$ - $8\frac{1}{2}$ in) in diameter although some examples had eight pointed flanges. Examples of third-century shield bosses found throughout the Empire mirror the Dura Europos finds, although examples of the eight pointed flange variety are rare and have few parallels. Constructed from either copper-alloy, which could be either spun or beaten, or iron, which could only be beaten into the correct shape, the shield boss could be either plain or decorated. The decoration could be either geometric, or figural, or a combination of both. Such decoration did not however, mark the object out as a piece of 'parade' equipment, it was designed for and would have been used on the battlefield.

The introduction of khaki at the end of the nineteenth century and the appearance of the scarlet coat only at events such as the Trooping of the Colour has very much coloured our view of the use of highly decorated items of military equipment in the Ancient World. However, up until the appearance of khaki; decoration, display, ornament, even show, were very much apart of how war was waged, and this was a truth understood as much by Napoleon Bonaparte as by any general in the Ancient World. Indeed, at Waterloo (1815) the French Army was remembered by those who took part, as being a scene of splendour, full of colour and polished metal.

Actual physical evidence for the continued use of the rectangular form of shield also comes from Dura Europos, where three examples were found. The best-preserved example came from Tower 19 and was 1.02m ($3\frac{1}{2}$ft) long, 0.83m ($2\frac{3}{4}$ft) wide, and 0.66m (2ft) along the chord of the arc. The method of construction employed can best be described as plywood in that it was made up from three superimposed layers. Each layer was made up of strips of plane wood 30-80mm (1-3in) wide and 15-20mm ($\frac{1}{2}$-$\frac{3}{4}$in) thick. The layers were glued together with the strips on the outer and inner layers running horizontally whilst those on the middle layer ran vertically, the overall thickness being approximately 50mm (2in). A circular hole, 120mm ($4\frac{1}{2}$in) was cut in the centre to accommodate the hand and a framework of pegged and glued horizontal and vertical wooden strips, 20mm ($\frac{3}{4}$in) wide was attached to the back; one strip which crossed the central aperture was strengthened and acted as a horizontal handgrip. The shield was covered on both sides by thin leather and the front was also covered with a layer of fine linen cloth. The rim had a stitched leather binding, 30-50mm ($1\frac{1}{3}$– 2 in) wide and the corners were reinforced with rawhide corner pieces. There were four holes for a rectangular flanged boss, which was missing.

Despite the wealth of archaeological evidence a number of gaps still exist. Hexagonal shields and the small circular shields used by standard-bearers and musicians in the first and second centuries, are absent from the archaeological record even though they are believed to have continued in use into the third century. Shield covers are also absent, but were in all probability used. There are also no definitely identified surviving examples of the training equipment used by the Army, the wicker shield found at Dura Europos, previously identified as a double weight training shield, being in all probability a Persian pavise.

3   *A third-century, copper-alloy shield boss from Mainz, Germany.*

    (Redrawn by K. R. Dixon from Thomas 1971)

Decoration on the majority of the Dura Europos shields was confined to painting in a single colour, pink. This is paralleled in the Synagogue representations where the individual shields in both the 'Exodus' and 'Battle of Ebenezer' frescoes are also painted in single colours, although, a greater range red/pink, blue, cream/white and brown, are used. Of the remaining finds whilst one was unpainted, three of the oval and one of the rectangular shields were quite richly adorned. Two of the ovals and the rectangular shield had red fields with concentric wreath, wavecrest and guilloche patterns around the boss. These were circular on the oval shields and square on the rectangular shield. On the main field one of the ovals contained scenes from the Iliad, whilst the other was decorated with an *Amazonomachy*. On the rectangular shield, the field above the concentric decoration contained an eagle flanked by two Victories, whilst that below held a lion flanked by two sun- or star-bursts. The remaining oval shield was painted grey-green and decorated with a full length figure dressed as a Palmyrene-style warrior god.

The backs of the shields were, with one exception, painted the same colour as the main field. The exception being the Amazon shield, which was painted blue and decorated with rosettes and radiating hearts (**colour plates 9 & 10**).

The purpose of such decoration was primarily practical, although it would contain an element of display. Tacitus in his description of the battle of Cremona AD 69 (Histories III.xxiii) and Ammianus Marcellinus in his description of the battle of Argentoratum (Strasburg) AD359 (XVI.12.6), both state that different units had different patterns or blazons on their shields. Vegetius, in his *Epitoma rei militaris* (II.18), written in the late-fourth/early-fifth century, also states that cohort specific designs were painted onto shields in order to facilitate unit differentiation and identification on the battlefield. However, any attempt to ascribe particular designs to particular units is at best problematic. Of the finds from Dura Europos the warrior god may well have been a unit emblem, as perhaps was the lion which may have belonged to a legionary detachment. The lions flanking sun- or star-bursts also appear on first- and second-century legionary blazons, thus further tying the lion to a legionary provenance. The meaning of the decoration, or lack of it, on the remaining shields, is unfortunately unknown.

The shield's effectiveness in battle was very much dependent upon both its method of construction and the type of weapons used against it. Although writing in the fourth century Ammianus' descriptions of the negating effects of artillery upon armour are still relevant in a third century context as the weapons used were identical. Ammianus XIX.1.7, XIX.5.6, and XXIV.4.28, describe respectively *ballista* bolts passing through chest and armour, such bolts piercing two men one after another, and the obliterating effects of a scorpion's stone shot, even in misfire. Although shields are not mentioned in any of these incidents, their presence or absence is an irrelevance, for artillery in the Roman period as in all periods nullified personal armour.

Equally effective, although only present during sieges were hand thrown stones. These stones, which were worked, are quite common finds from military sites throughout the Empire. They were a classical jam doughnut shape, weighing approximately 0.7-1.0kg and fitted comfortably in the palm of the hand. As a weapon they are mentioned as early as the fourth century BC by Aeneas in his work *On the Defence of Fortified Position*; they should not however, be confused with the stones mentioned by Dio LXXV.6 which were used in pitched battle and which were in all probability merely picked from the ground with little thought to shape or size. As to their effectiveness, the hand thrown stone was more than capable of reducing a shield to splinters and experiment has shown that this could be achieved in a very short space of time, as the weapon permits a very high rate of 'fire'.

In battle the air was filled with missiles; javelins, arrows and slingshot (Dio LXXV.6 and LXXVI.6 Herodian VI.5.9), and against these weapons the shield was a more than effective defence. The disaster which befell a Roman army at the hands of the Persians (Herodian VI.5.9) was not, as indeed Herodian states, a result of the Romans having inadequate protection against the arrows of the Persians, but was rather a result of the fact that a small Roman force was surrounded by a far larger one.

Whilst the effects of the *pila* volley upon barbarian hordes is often considered, its effect upon Roman armies is not. Yet in times of civil war, legionary and auxiliary units could well be on the receiving end of such a volley. Properly used against barbarians (Caesar, Gallic War I.25 and VII.62) such an attack could be devastating. However, against fellow Romans the picture is complicated by both a greatly increased level of armour provision and a variety of shield construction techniques. The plank method of construction, adopted in the third century, was no match for the *pilum*, and the most troops equipped with this type of shield could hope for was a premature volley, which would mean that the *pilum* lacked sufficient energy to pierce the combined layers of shield, body armour, *thoracomachus* and clothing. However, the plywood method of construction should, in theory, have protected the infantryman against a *pila* volley even if delivered at extreme close range, 10m or less.

The skirmishing and missile exchange phases, at the beginning of an engagement, saw the shield used solely in a defensive role. The next phase, which began with the sides closing to contact and which culminated in hand-to-hand combat, required the shield to be used both defensively and offensively. Defensively, although missiles may still be raining down, the main threats against which the shield was now deployed came from the spears, swords, and in some cases axes of the enemy.

The hurly-burly of hand-to-hand combat and the destructive power of the weapons used, is unfortunately not a theme of the writing of the period, being more a leitmotif of later Germanic writers and it is to these, particularly Anglo-Saxon and Viking sources, that we must turn in order to gain some picture of the shields effectiveness. For if the plank shield was new to the Roman Army in the third century, the same was not true of their Germanic enemies, for whom it was the standard method of construction in both the Roman and Germanic Iron Ages, and also into the Viking Age. The shield in Germanic literature could be pierced by spear and cleft by sword and axe. Leaving aside poetic exaggeration, as the plank shield was not a perfect defence, this in all probability reflected actuality in both the Roman and Germanic worlds. Sufficient force could be put into a spear thrust to allow the spear to penetrate the shield and blows from swords and axes could shatter the planks. However, from the defender's point of view, the shield, as can be seen in the reconstructions, covered most of the body and was an obstacle which the attacker not only had to get either through, past or around, but which also required him to expend energy in order to achieve this end. It was, as far as the defender was concerned, far better to have the attacker exhaust himself in destroying this wooden obstacle than in destroying himself. The very size of the shield also worked in the defender's favour in another way; a small shield requires the user to be both constantly vigilant and constantly moving the shield to block blows, whereas a large shield, by providing practically complete coverage of the body reduces the amount of movement required, and the amount of energy expended. It also provides a degree of unconscious coverage against ill-aimed blows delivered from the periphery of the defender's field of vision.

The sheer size and weight of the shield did not however, make it a ponderous, unwieldy item. Constant training including battlefield simulations, with both double and single weight shields, gave the Roman infantryman the stamina, confidence and ability to use the shield offensively. Although the shield itself could not deliver a killing blow it could facilitate such a blow. A punching blow with the boss or a pushing blow using the shield as a whole, could unbalance an opponent and cause him to drop his guard sufficiently to allow the attacker to deliver a fatal blow or series of blows.

Plywood construction imparted a far greater degree of battlefield resilience than its plank equivalent, and although plywood construction is more commonly associated with the rectangular design of shield, a fragment of an oval plywood shield was found at Dura Europos. The third-century infantryman was required to operate in both close order and skirmish formation, and to move seamlessly between the two. The rectangular design, unlike the oval or hexagonal, was limited in its use, being purpose built solely for close order combat. Although it continued in use, certainly until the mid-third century, it does not appear to have survived into the fourth century.

A final question which must be asked in connection with the shield is — what was the life span of the shield? Metallic body armour could, if damaged, be repaired; it could also be passed on to other users, following the original owner's departure, either by death or discharge, from the army. Indeed, helmets have been found in the archaeological record inscribed with more than one name, implying continuous use over both a number of years and a number of owners. Yet is the same true of shields? The answer is no and yes. No, in terms of the shield as a whole, yes in terms of its metal fittings. The shield as a whole had a limited life, which although unquantifiable, as the effects of general wear and tear would vary from shieldboard to shieldboard, was in all probability less than a soldier's term of service. Thus, a soldier be he a legionary or auxiliary, even if he never saw action, would have gone through more than one shieldboard in the course of his 20 or 25 years service.

The use of the term shieldboard is important as it allows a distinction to be drawn between the shield as a whole and the wooden body or board of the shield. For once a shieldboard was damaged in any way it became useless, the metal fittings (the boss and the grip) would then be stripped from the board and the board discarded. The metal fittings could then be either reattached to a new board, repaired first if necessary or recycled if too badly damaged to reattach. This process could, potentially be massively accelerated if the soldier saw action. Participation in an action, be it a small skirmish or full scale pitched battle, exposes the shield to the weapons of the enemy, even though in itself the shield is not the target, for as the soldier's first line of defence it should, in theory, bear the brunt of any attack. If during such an action the shield were hit, then, no matter how minor the damage, the shieldboard would be scrapped. It would not be repaired and only the metal fittings would be salvaged. This may seem a little extreme, not to say wasteful, but from the soldier's point of view the shield was compromised, fatally and irretrievably. He could not trust his life to it, thus any continued use after the action would only result in the soldier operating with a lowered morale, and soldiers with low morale lose battles. Exactly the same reasoning was applied to the scrapping of shieldboards as a result of accidental damage. The infantrymen of the day trusted his life more to his shield than to any other piece of equipment and in order to maintain that trust the Army saw the shield in many ways in the same light as the spear and the javelin — it was disposable.

3 Helmets

The heads of others were split through mid forehead and crown with
swords and hung down on both shoulders, a most horrible sight.

Ammianus Marcellinus, XXXI.7.14

The helmet designs of the first and second centuries were discontinued in the
third and a new style of infantry helmet appeared. However, whilst this new style
maybe seen as a departure in design terms from its predecessors, the style did
follow the general trend of the preceding centuries by further increasing the level
of protection afforded to the head.

This new style of helmet, typified by an example found at Heddernheim,
Germany (**fig 4, colour plate 14 & cover**), in general had a bowl of either iron
or copper alloy, which extended down to the base of the neck, where there was an
angled neckguard. On the front of the bowl there was a pointed peak, which could
be either horizontal or upwardly angled. Over the crown and extending to the
base of the neck were crossed reinforcing bars. Both the peak and crossed
reinforcing bars were attached using decorative cone shaped, or dome headed
rivets. The cheek-pieces were large, and over lapped on the chin, leaving only a
small 'T'-shaped face opening. The cheek-pieces were hinged along their upper
edge. They fastened via a hook on the front of the left cheek-piece passing
through a hole on the front of the right cheek-piece. A variation on this form is
provided by an incomplete example found at Buch, Germany (**colour plate 7**),
which would have been fitted with a peak but which would not have had crossed
reinforcing bars, as instead it had embossed cross-ribs.

The use of crossed reinforcing bars, and the absence of both forked crest-box
holders and plume-tubes in the archaeological record, point not only to a change
in fashion but also to a change in priorities. Display had become subordinate to
protection.

Helmets of both types appear on a small number of third-century gravestones,
including that of an armoured legionary (?) from Brigetio, Hungary, and the
tombstone of Aurelius Surus, Istanbul. They also appear on the decorative *phalera*
of Aurelius Cervianus and on a number of the Dura Europos Synagogue frescoes.

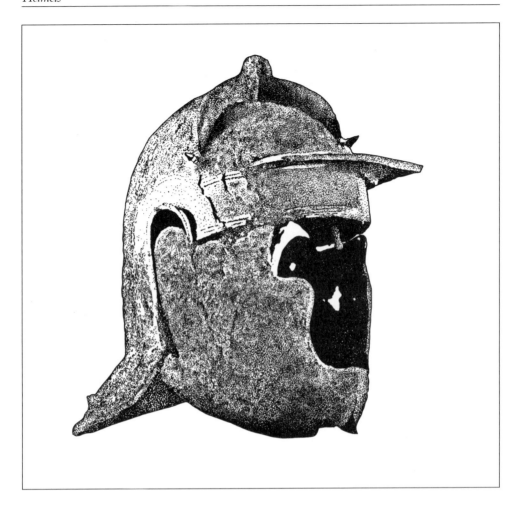

4   *Helmet from Heddernheim, Germany*

(Drawn by K. R. Dixon)

Despite the emergence of this new style of helmet there would have been some degree of continuance into the third century of the older 'Imperial' styles. Conical helmets, found on Danubian sites, can also be dated to the late second/early third centuries (**colour plate 11**). The example illustrated in the reconstruction of the archer, is fitted with a mail curtain, which although more normally associated with the medieval period, is paralleled both in Assyrian art and by a mid-third century find of a Persian helmet from Dura Europos.

Another form of protective headgear, again more commonly associated with the medieval period, but which was also employed by the Roman Army in the third century was the coif (**colour plate 8**). No examples survive, and the representational evidence is limited to two examples, one from the third century (the 'Battle of Ebenezer' fresco, Dura Europos), and another from the fourth century (the *Vergilius Vaticanus* manuscript)(**fig 5**). Neither are sufficiently detailed to categorically state their method of construction, although the Dura Europos fresco probably depicts scale coifs, whereas the *Vergilius Vaticanus* are more likely to be of mail; both methods are practicable and both methods were probably used.

It is axiomatic that the head provides one of the main target areas in combat. A blow to the head if not immediately fatal, will more than likely render the recipient *hors de combat*. The shield can provide some protection but it is fleeting and transitory, limited to intercepting seen blows aimed at the face or raised above the head in the rear ranks of a shieldwall to protect against the missile storm. The main means of protecting the head is of course the helmet, and the infantry helmet in the third century, as typified by the Heddernheim and Buch examples, provided this protection on a number of different levels.

The main preventable threats came from either in front; from thrust, slash, or missile; or from above, from missile weapons. Therefore in order to maximise protection the exposed area of the face on third-century helmets was reduced to a small 'T'-shaped area which equated to the eyes, nose and mouth. The curved cheek-pieces acted as a glancing surface, protecting against thrusts and missiles, whilst both the curve of the bowl and sloping neckguard provided effective glancing surface protection against missile weapons, such as arrows and javelins.

Defence against slashing blows was provided by either the peak or a combination of the peak and crossed reinforcing bars. The principle behind this defence being quite straightforward, the crossed reinforcing bars and/or peak basically intercepted the blow and prevented it contacting the bowl where it would have the potential to inflict damage. The simplicity of this design, indeed the helmet itself, would however, be for nought if some form of padding were not employed.

A successful blow to an unpadded helmet would cause either concussion in the best case, or blunt trauma and its associated internal haemorrhaging in the worst. Padding could prevent this; the extra layers it provides between the helmet and head, both absorb and dissipate the force of the blow, greatly reducing the amount of damage caused. Unfortunately the means of padding is unknown to us. The padding could be worn either as a hat, under the helmet; or fastened to the inside to the helmet. The former is more likely, as surviving third-century helmets both lack evidence of padding and any visible means of attachment. Corroborating the hat as a means of padding is the fourth century author and soldier, Ammianus Marcellinus, who states that a cap was worn under the helmet (XIX.8.8); and is there is no reason to believe that helmet padding materially differed between the third and fourth centuries AD, this further pushes the balance of probabilities towards a hat and away from an internal helmet liner.

As to the design of the hat, two possibilities present themselves. Firstly, the *pilleus*, the sheepskin pillbox hat more commonly associated with the Tetrarchy, than the earlier third century, could have been used (**colour plate 2**). Indeed experiments by The Arbeia Society have shown that it makes an effective padding

5   *Armoured infantrymen from the fourth-century* Vergilius Vaticanus *manuscript.*

(Redrawn by K. R. Dixon from Coulston 1990)

for a helmet. Secondly, a more medieval style, padded and quilted cloth arming cap could have been worn. Both types are practicable and both may very well have been used.

The coif is in many ways a less effective form of protection, although this did not prevent its use well into the medieval period in both Europe and Islam. There is, however, no evidence for the medieval practice of wearing a helmet over the coif.

Of the two possible variants used, scale coifs would have offered a greater degree of protection against both thrusts and missiles, as mail is particularly vulnerable to these types of attack. Both types would have provided the same level of protection against slashing blows. However, and this would be due in part to the lack of peak and reinforcing bars, it would be of a lower level of protection than that provided by a helmet. The coif would also have required at least the same level of padding as a helmet. Where the coif wins over the helmet is in protecting the throat. The coif by its very design automatically covers this area, whereas a helmeted soldier must wear a gorget to protect his throat.

4 *Thoracomachus*

Gay gowns of grene
To hold thayr armur clene
And were it from the wete

The Avowing of King Arthur. *c.1200*

The *thoracomachus* (*De Rebus Bellicis* XV)(**fig 6**) or *subarmalis* (*Scriptores Historiae Augustae* VI.11), the words may well be synonyms, was a vital part of the soldier's equipment, indeed he could not operate in the field without it. The best, near contemporary, description of the *thoracomachus* comes from the late-fourth/early-fifth century, Anonymous, *De Rebus Bellicis* (XV), which describes it as being a garment of thick cloth, which had three functions. These were: to act as added protection for the body, to counteract the weight and friction of the armour, and to allow the wearer to function more efficiently in cold weather. The first being its primary function, the others being secondary benefits.

In order to perform all of these functions the garment was in all probability padded, being made either from a number of layers of cloth (wool, felt or linen) sewn together; or alternatively from two layers of cloth stuffed with scraps of wool (or another fabric), and then vertically quilted. The latter method is the same as that employed in the construction of the medieval *gambeson* and *aketon* and indeed they performed the same functions as their earlier equivalents the *thoracomachus* and *subarmalis* (**colour plate 2**).

Its primary function, as has already been stated, was to act as added protection for the body by being worn under the armour and the *De Rebus Bellicis* implies that it was used in conjunction with all armour types. Yet this does not tell us the why of the matter.

Armour will stop a cutting/slashing or concussive blow, and plate armour also provides a high level of proof against a penetrative thrust. However, the force of the blow must be considered, as this can also cause injury, and the inadequacy of some armour types in protecting the wearer against penetrating thrusts is a further factor which must be borne in mind,

A cutting, slashing or concussive blow does not need to break through the armour in order to cause damage — contact is enough. For if the blow is dealt with sufficient force, then this force will be transferred through the armour causing, in what is known as 'a blunt trauma injury', broken bones and internal

6   Thoracomachus *and 'Libyan hide', hanging on a wooden frame. From the editio princeps manuscript of* De Rebus Bellicis.

(Drawn by M. Daniels)

haemorrhaging. The wearing of padding under the armour at best prevents this, or at worst reduces the severity of the blunt trauma. It does this by absorbing the force of the blow, something which armour alone cannot do.

Thrusting blows from spears and arrows can also cause blunt trauma injuries. This was especially true if the victim was wearing plate or scale armour, which were less susceptible to penetration. Where penetration did occur, and this was more likely in the case of mail (although it could also occur with both plate and scale) then the main priority was to prevent deep penetration. If penetration occurred in the abdomen then it was highly probable that the intestines would be punctured, resulting in peritonitis and thus death. Whereas if penetration of the chest cavity occurred, then the likely results were sepsis and death.

Again, as with the prevention of blunt trauma injuries the best method of preventing deep penetrating wounds was to use under-armour padding. In the Roman Armies' case this took the form of the *thoracomachus*. Although not fully proof, it did increase the soldier's level of protection. It worked against penetrative blows, in much the same way as it worked against blunt traumas, namely by dissipating the force of the blow. Part of the power of the blow was used to pierce the armour, the *thoracomachus* then took more power out of the blow, by virtue of it being a dense layer through which the weapon had to pass. The soldier's tunic was then the next layer that had to be pierced; with the whole effect, armour, *thoracomachus*, tunic, being cumulative. Thus in theory even if the weapon did actually contact the skin, there should not have been enough force left in it to allow it to achieve its objective — a fatal, deep penetrative wound.

One drawback with the *thoracomachus* was that the soldier was expected to operate under arms in wet weather, and in wet weather the *thoracomachus* became, as it soaked up the water, heavy and burdensome. This would have had a detrimental effect on the soldier's morale and would have impaired his operational ability. In order to prevent this a leather over-garment was worn. According to Anonymous, *De Rebus Bellicis* XV, this garment was made of Libyan hide. The garment itself was the same shape, if slightly larger than the *thoracomachus*, and the term Libyan hide was probably a synonym.

As to the purpose of this leather tunic, it was designed to allow the soldier to operate under arms in wet weather. As wet weather, even in Northern Europe, is not constant, then the tunic was probably carried by the soldier and only worn when absolutely necessary. The *De Rebus Bellicis* (XV) tells us in rather general terms that the tunic of Libyan hide was worn over the *thoracomachus*, it is not however, specific and does not say whether it was worn over or under the armour. The most sensible solution is to have such a garment worn over the armour, necessitating only the removal of the sword, dagger/short sword and helmet in order to put on. This would also allow it to protect the armour as well as the *thoracomachus* from the elements, and parallels may be drawn with the medieval surcoat which performed a similar function in protecting armour from the weather (**colour plate 10**).

The helmet may also have had a protective, wet weather covering. Although no contemporary evidence exists, the Emperor Maurice, AD 582-602, recommends the use of a hooded felt cloak or mantle (*Strategikon*, I.2) to protect the armour from rain and damp. It is thus possible that a helmet covering was employed in the third century, although it may only have been used on iron helmets. The second use of the cloak, (*Strategikon*, I.2) was to prevent helmet and armour reflecting the sun whilst out on patrol. This was however, more a feature of cavalry equipment, being paralleled in the Napoleonic period by the oilskin helmet covers worn by dragoons for the same purpose.

5 Mail and scale

And there marched on either side twin lines of infantrymen
with shields and crests gleaming with glittering rays,
clad in shining mail.

Ammianus Marcellinus, XVI.10.8

There are unfortunately few reliable representations of body armour for the third
century. The general fashion on military tombstones of the period was to show the
deceased unarmoured. In a few cases, the dead soldier was depicted surrounded by
his equipment, and in these cases the defensive equipment normally depicted was
helmet and shield. There are, however, two exceptions. The first exception is the
tombstone of Severius Acceptus, Istanbul, which as well as depicting the helmet
and shield, also shows a pair of greaves and some form of armour(?), although this
may in fact be either a form of composite armour or a *thoracomachus*. The second
is that of Aurelius Antipators of *legio IV Scythica*, Iznik, Turkey, who again was
depicted with his helmet, but also with a diminutive suit of armour.

Staying with funerary monuments, the mid-third-century Great Ludovisi
Battle Sarcophagus, Rome, has a very nicely executed depiction of mail, but
unfortunately, the work as a whole is rather conservative and adds nothing to our
knowledge of third-century armour. The same is also true of the Arch of Severus,
Rome, which is one of the few monumental propaganda sculptures of the period.
The Arch depicts soldiers in mail, scale and *lorica segmentata*, but is very conservative
in execution, with the carvings owing more to the Marcus Column, in terms of
their stylistic depictions of the Army, than to the reality of the day. The death of
Septimius Severus, in AD 211, led, for obvious political reasons, to a
discontinuance in the construction of these propaganda monuments. This
discontinuance only ended at the close of the third century with the accession of
Diocletian in AD 284.

However, despite this, accurate representations of fully armoured third-century
Roman infantrymen do exist. An anonymous tombstone(?) from Brigetio,
Hungary, and the Synagogue frescoes from Dura Europos, Syria, both show
armoured soldiers, and it is from these that we have gained our understanding of
the style of armour prevailing in the third century.

7   *The 'Battle of Ebenezer' fresco from the Synagogue, Dura Europos, Syria.*

(Drawn by M. Daniels)

The figure on the Brigetio tombstone and the figures in the 'Battle of Ebenezer' and 'Exodus' frescoes where knee length armour, of mail(?) in the case of Brigetio and mail(?) and scale(?) in the Dura Europos examples. In both cases the armour was sleeved, and the sleeves were shown as being either elbow length (Bregetio) or wrist length (Dura Europos)(**figs 7 & 8**). Corroboration for the continuance of this style through into the fourth century, comes from a relief of two soldiers. The relief is believed to have belonged to the now lost Arch of Diocletian, Rome, and is currently in the Vatican Museo Chiaramonti (**fig 9**). The relief which has been dated to the late third/early fourth century, depicts two soldiers both wearing conical helmets and carrying large round shields and spears. The figure on the left wears mail whilst the one on the right is dressed in scale. In both cases the armour has wrist length sleeves and was probably knee length, although the lower legs are missing.

If the representational evidence can best be described as meagre when compared to the earlier Imperial period, the same can not be said of the archaeological evidence.

Finds of partial and complete mail shirts occur throughout the Empire; with examples coming from Caerleon and South Shields, in Great Britain; Bertoldsheim, Kunzing, Grosskrotzenburg and Buch in Germany; Dura Europos, Syria; and beyond, the Danish Vimose shirt being probably Roman in origin. The mail itself could be either copper-alloy (Grosskrotzenburg), or more normally iron, or a combination of both, as in the case of the example found at

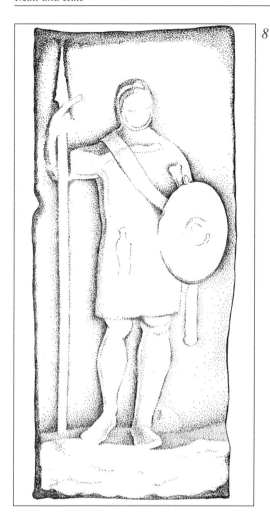

8   *The tombstone(?) of an amoured legionary(?) from Brigetio, Hungary.*

(Drawn by M. Daniels)

Bertoldsheim (**colour plate 3**). The rings themselves tended, on average, to be of a similar size, both throughout the Empire and across the period as a whole, namely 7mm external diameter and 1mm thick. The construction technique employed was one of alternate rows of solid, either welded or stamped, rings and riveted rings.

   Finds of scale armour are equally common, with noteworthy examples coming from Dura Europos, Syria; Straubing, Germany; and particularly Carpow, Great Britain (**colour plate 4**). The Carpow find, although not a complete set, is important as the surviving section of scale retains its textile backing and is thus very informative in terms of constructional detail. The find is probably Severan in date, with the scales being of copper-alloy, 15mm long and 13mm wide. Each scale was pierced by six holes, two in the centre at the top and two slightly lower down on the right and left edges of the scale. Each scale was wired to its neighbour, to the left and right through these side holes, forming strips of scales. These strips were then secured to both a horizontal linen cord and the linen backing of the

9   *Late third/early fourth century armoured infantrymen, possibly from the Arch of Diocletian(?), Rome.*

(Redrawn by K. R. Dixon from Coulston 1990)

armour by linen thread (**fig 10**). A decorative, and not uncommon feature of scale armour was achieved using tinning. Alternate scales could be tinned so as to produce a gold and silver checker board pattern. Conversely the whole garment could be made up of tinned scales to produce a silver fish scale effect.

A feature of both mail and scale armour was the use of embossed copper-alloy breastplates. Despite their decorative nature they were not pieces of 'sports /parade' equipment, but were for use in the field and served a very practical purpose. They were designed to act as closure plates, giving the armour a tight protective fit at the neck. They were introduced in the second century as a replacement for the earlier shoulder doubling, hook fastening combination of the late Republic and early Empire. These plates were of two different types. The more common type was made up of two equally sized plates which had an average length of 15cm and a width of 7.9cm. They were attached to the armour via rivet holes along their outside edges, and were curved on the upper edge in order to fit around the neck. They were fastened by square headed pins which passed through slots on each plate and which were themselves held in place by a rod. The second form, typified by an example from Bertoldsheim was again made up of two asymmetrical copper-alloy plates which together form a trapezoid 14cm long, 6.4cm wide at the bottom (the main plate being 5.3cm at this point), and 5cm

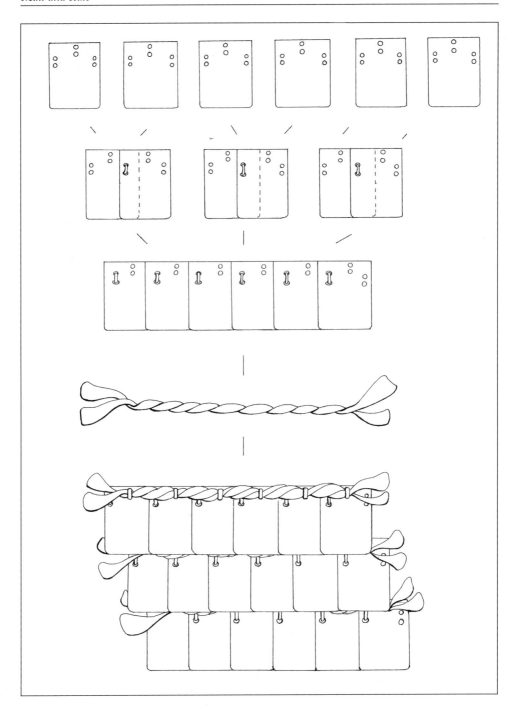

10   *A diagram illustrating the construction of the Carpow scale armour.*

(Redrawn by M. Daniels from Coulston 1992)

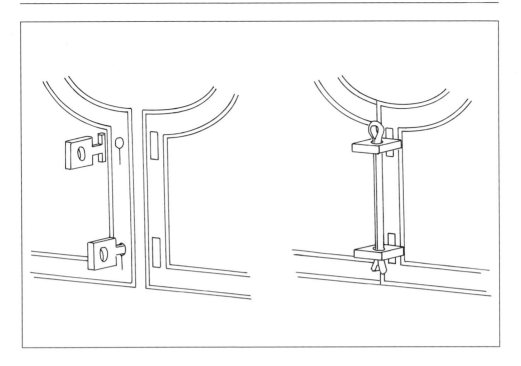

11   A diagram showing how the symmetrical breastplates fastened.

(Redrawn by J. R. A. Underwood from Garbsch 1978)

wide at the top (with the main plate being 3.9cm wide at this point), the other plate being approximately 1.1cm wide for the whole of its length. The plates were curved on the upper edge in order to fit around the neck and fastened using a hook and catch-plate system. The centre of the left hand edge of the main plate was extended to form a hook, whilst a slot in the other plate allowed it to act as a catch-plate (**fig 11**).

The mail shirt was a relatively straightforward garment, and our understanding of it is greater than our understanding of its scale equivalent. The mail shirt was a single garment, the sleeves were integral and tight necked closure was achieved via the use of Bertoldsheim type plates (**fig 12 & colour plate 3**). The scale shirt, however, is not so straightforward; for it is not known how such armour was put on, nor how the sleeves were attached.

In terms of putting on a number of possibilities present themselves; the scale shirt could either open solely down one side, or it could open down one side and one shoulder; or it could open down the back; or down the front; or finally with no openings other than the obvious neck arms and bottom, the scale shirt could be put on in the same way as mail. All of the above methods are practicable, however, the methods which employed front, back or side openings would have also required some form of fastening mechanism (either buckles or ties) in order

12   *The breastplate from Bertoldsheim, Germany.*

(Drawn by M. Daniels)

to securely close these openings. Side and shoulder openings would have been on the left hand side only, thus allowing the shield to cover these obvious weak points, and would have the advantage over the back opening in allowing the soldier to easily do up his own fastenings. The full front opening may seem bizarre, but a complete Chinese example does exist. Finally, the mail shirt method. Here the scale would be just put on over the head, thus doing away with the need for buckles or ties and their attendant weaknesses. The practicality of all of these systems is not questioned; the representational evidence is too poor to provide any clues as to which if any, were used. The archaeological evidence may, however, provide a clue as to which was used. Scale, like mail, used decorative copper-alloy plates to ensure a tight fit at the neck (**colour plate 4**); such plates would not be necessary if shoulder, back or front openings were employed. Therefore the balance of probabilities lies with the single left side opening and the no openings methods, both of which may well have been used.

Sleeves on mail were, as has already been stated, integral. The same was probably not true of their scale counterparts, as integral scale sleeves would inhibit movement. Experiments by The Arbeia Society have shown that wrist length scale sleeves are quite feasible. They have also demonstrated that the easiest method of attachment is to have the sleeves separate to the main body attached by shoulder ties, with any gap covered by a combination of the shoulders on the main body of the shirt and *pteruges* (protective strips, made up of a number of layers of linen, which were either glued or sewn together)(**colour plates 4 & 6**).

The relative levels of protection offered by different types of armour has to a large extent already been covered (see above under *'Thoracomachus'*); however, it is worth reiterating in specific terms for mail and scale. In the majority of cases both mail and scale would stop or deflect a cutting or slashing blow, although it was certainly possible to deliver a blow with sufficient force to cut through metal body armour. Against both spears and arrows, mail is a less than adequate defence, and a blow landed on target, with sufficient force, from one of these weapons could seriously compromise the integrity of the mail. The links could be burst apart by such a thrusting blow, with potentially fatal consequences for the wearer. Scale, by presenting more of a glancing surface, gave a relatively greater degree of protection against such blows, but was not fully proof against this form of attack and could be pierced.

Despite this seeming superiority of scale over mail, mail did in fact have two advantages over scale, namely its flexibility and its durability. The armpit is a vulnerable area, and a successful blow to this area is at best incapacitating. Although both mail and scale were sleeved, fully integral sleeves were only practicable with mail, and it was only this type of sleeve which could provide armoured protection for the vulnerable armpit. Scale was too inflexible to provide such protection, and as the sleeves were separate, the best that could be done to protect this area was to use *pteruges*.

As to durability, scale would have been far more susceptible to daily wear and tear than mail. An act of force was required to remove rings from a mail shirt, whereas individual scales could be lost by threads wearing through and wires being accidentally snapped. Thus scale requires constant care and attention, and soldiers equipped with such armour in all probability carried around their own repair kit of spare scales, wire, needle, thread, and backing cloth. Mail although harder to break was not so easily fixed. This was not however a problem for the Imperial Roman Army, for even on a campaign it had its own artificers ready at hand.

Before going on to consider the frequency and distribution by unit type of mail and scale, the use of solid scale should be considered. This variation on standard scale was introduced in the second century. Here the scales were long and slender, and each scale was pierced by four sets of holes. The holes were in vertical pairs, with a single pair on each edge of the scale. The scales as well as being wired to their neighbour on each side were also wired to the scale above and below, forming a rigid or solid defence. No complete examples survive, however, due to its method of construction it is believed that it was only used as a torso defence and indeed reconstructions by The Arbeia Society have shown that such torso armour is perfectly feasible.

Mail, as has already been stated, was vulnerable to thrusts both from arrows and spears. This was partly compensated against by wearing a padded undergarment, the *thoracomachus*. Yet it could also be militated against by wearing a rigid defence over the mail, and this is the perceived use of solid scale in the third century. It was worn as an extra layer of torso armour over mail by both infantry and cavalry, to provide an increased level of effective protection at both the individual and unit level (**colour plates 9 & 11**).

As to the frequency and distribution of mail and scale they were the standard armour types in use in the third century. They were used equally by both legionary and auxiliary troops throughout the whole Empire. The only caveat is that during the third century scale became co-equal with the muscled cuirass on representations of generals and Emperors.

6 *Lorica Segmentata*

It is well armed with a thick skin,
and is very frolicsome
and in good condition.

Albrecht Dürer. 1513

The depiction of *lorica segmentata* on the Arch of Severus, Rome, *c*.AD203, coupled with the lack of archaeological and representational evidence for later in the third century, led to the belief that this form of armour did not continue in use after the early third century. Indeed it was believed that it had begun to be phased out in the late second century. However, in recent years this picture has changed, not as a result of new representational finds (although this has occurred) but rather as a result of new archaeological evidence. Finds from Carlisle, Great Britain, but more especially from the temple site at Eining, Germany (constructed *c*.AD 226/229, abandoned *c*.AD 260) show that *lorica segmentata* continued in use, potentially right through until the middle of the third century. As to the new representational evidence, an unusual statue from Alba Iulia, Romania, which shows a legionary (?) wearing this form of armour can unfortunately only be dated, imprecisely, to the late second/early third centuries.

The style of *lorica segmentata* worn during the third century followed the pattern set in the second century, under the Antonines, when the Newstead type was introduced as a replacement for the earlier Corbridge types. The Newstead type was far simpler in construction (**fig 13**). The semi-functional hinges on the shoulder plates and chest had been removed, as had the buckles and decorative rosettes. The breast plates now employed a fastening mechanism similar to that used on the decorative mail and scale closures, and the Corbridge type tie hooks had been replaced by simple loops. However, the attachment of the upper and lower halves of the armour used the same method (a sort of hook and eye system) as that employed on the Corbridge B type.

As to the degree of use, *lorica segmentata* remained confined to the legions in the third century (**fig 14**), as it had in previous centuries, although it was far less ubiquitous than in earlier periods. Despite the move in this period to a lack of differentiation between legionary and auxiliary equipment, there is no evidence to suggest that *lorica segmentata* was ever used by auxiliary units.

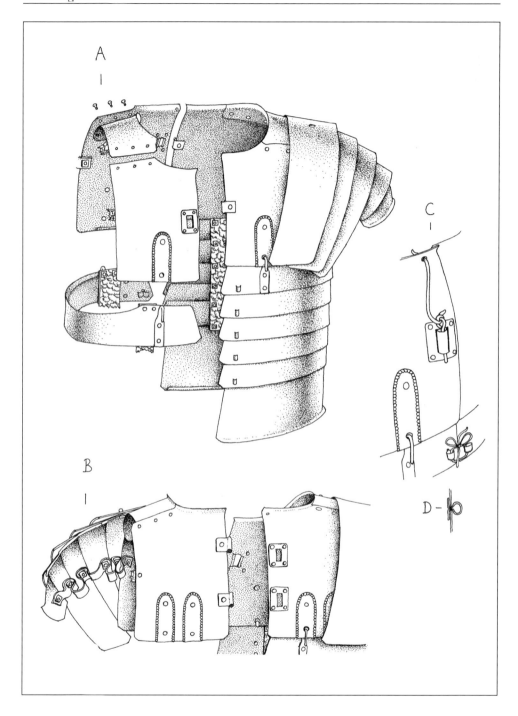

13   *The Newstead type* lorica segmentata. *A: Front, B: Back, C: Breastplate and girdle closure mechanisms, D: Section through girdle plate showing fastener.*

(Redrawn by M. Daniels from Connolly)

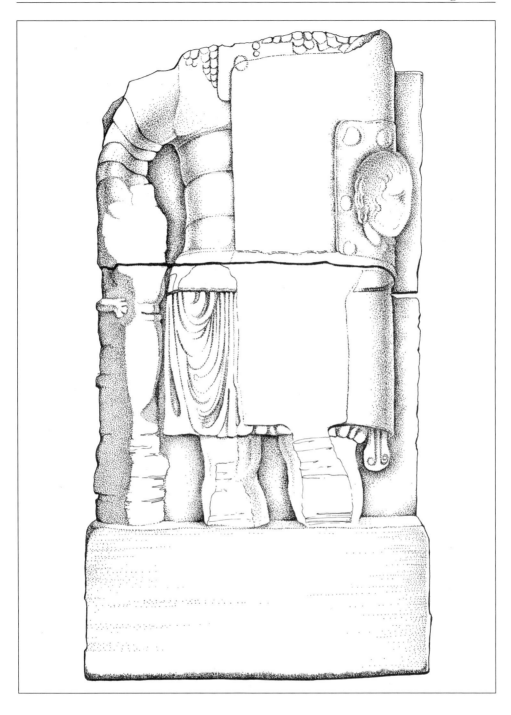

14 *An armoured legionary from Alba Iulia, Romania.*

(Drawn by M. Daniels)

There is also no evidence to suggest that *lorica segmentata* continued in use later than the third century. As to why this should be, two reasons present themselves — neither of which are definitive and both probably worked in conjunction with each other. Firstly, *lorica segmentata*, even the simplified Newstead type, was over-engineered. It required high levels of maintenance due to the combination of internal leather straps and the use of mixed metal fittings which acted as rust traps. It was thus harder to produce and more importantly harder to maintain, especially during a period when warfare had become endemic and the relative time the soldiers spent in the field had increased. Secondly, only the upper body of the soldier was protected. The stomach, chest and shoulders may have been protected by glancing surfaces, but the arms and the rest of the body from the waist down were unprotected. This made this form of armour incompatible with a period where armour was being worn to a far greater degree (in terms of body coverage) than in previous centuries.

7 Greaves

Therefore he said that a man on starting for a review or a campaign should
in putting on his greaves take more care to see that they fit well and look
shiny than he does about his shoes and boots.

Polybius, XI.9.4

The protection of the legs from the waist to the knees was not a problem; this area
being covered by both the body armour and shield. The foot was not a major
target area and was not armoured. However, the shins and calves which were
vulnerable to attack were not covered by the body armour, nor could they be
adequately protected by a downward movement of the shield, as such a move
would expose the upper body to attack.

For light infantry (javelineers, archers, and skirmishers) lack of protection was
not a problem, as armour was sacrificed for speed. However, for the heavy
infantryman fighting in close-order this lack of protection could prove fatal. As a
blow to the shin or calves although not in itself fatal, unless the leg was completely
severed, could prove debilitating enough to allow the soldier's guard to slip —
thus opening him up for a killing blow. To prevent this, and indeed to provide a
completely armoured frontage from head to foot, greaves were worn (**colour
plates 5, 12 & 13**).

However, before considering the style and type of greaves used, the question of
who wore them and when they were worn shall be considered. Initially it was
believed that, in of terms of infantry usage, greaves were the preserve of the
Centurionate. However, a number of factors make this interpretation unlikely.
Firstly, greaves are used by ordinary soldiers on the Adamklissi metopes; secondly,
Vegetius believed (I.20) that at least one greave (probably worn on the left leg) was
standard equipment for the legionary; thirdly, their depiction on a third century
legionary gravestone, that of Severius Acceptus, Istanbul; and finally, all of the
front rank soldiers in the 'Exodus' fresco from Dura Europos are probably
wearing greaves (**fig 15**). Thus the evidence points to a far wider use than was
initially supposed.

Indeed if a comparison is drawn with the Hoplite phalanx in Classical Age
Greece, then we will see that greaves were standard pieces of equipment, and
given the fact that both the Greek Hoplite and the third-century Roman

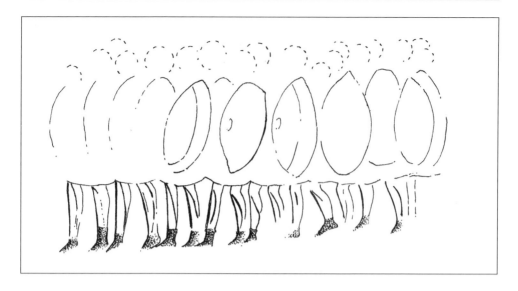

15   A detail of the 'Exodus' fresco from the Synagogue, Dura Europos, Syria. Of particular note are the greaves worn by all the figures.

(Drawn by M. Daniels)

infantryman participated in close-order 'decisive battle' with much the same weapons, then a wider use of greaves by the Romans seems probable.

As to the style and types worn, the plain iron greaves found at Kunzing, Germany, probably provide the best evidence for the type worn by the Roman infantryman of the third century. They are, as has been stated, plain iron, and were 33.5cm long, V-sectioned, with straight flanges on the upper and lower edges and double raised hollows on each side. Unlike the snap fit greaves of the Classical Period these have four attachments, to each side, four tie rings, which would presumably have had leather ties attached. Copper-alloy greaves were also worn, with fragments being found at Dura Europos. A linen greave lining was also found at Dura Europos although we need not assume that all greaves were lined.

Embossed greaves are also found, however; they are usually made with both ankle and knee guards and are thus assumed to be cavalry equipment. One exception to this is a piece recovered from the Rhine at Speyer, dated to the late second/early third centuries, decorated with an embossed figure of Mars. This may well be a piece of cavalry equipment, although it is probably more plausible to view it as a piece of infantry equipment due to the lack of knee and ankle guards.

8 Gorget

For the Lord Clifford, either from heat or pain, put off his gorget, was suddenly hit by an arrow, as some say, without a head and was stricken in the throat, and rendered up his spirit.

Hall's Chronicle. c.1540

The gorget or collar, as it was also known in the medieval period, was a defence for the neck, the extreme top of the chest and the shoulders. The evidence for its use by the Roman Army of the third century comes from one of the few depictions from this period of an armoured soldier. The Brigetio figure (possibly a legionary — the gravestone lacks an inscription) wears knee length, elbow-length armour, a helmet with the angled peak, flaring neck guard and wide cheek pieces typical of the third century, and most importantly a collar which covers the throat as well as the top of the chest and shoulders of the figure. Indeed, it fills the normally unarmoured gap between the armour and the helmet. It is this collar, which fulfils the role of, and is indeed believed to represent, a metallic gorget.

As to the construction of the artifact, although we do not know how it was constructed, three possible methods present themselves; mail, scale, or plate. One parallel, and indeed it is probably not too wide of the mark, is a scale example, dated to the fourth century BC from Derveni, Greece (**colour plate 5**). The Derveni gorget was made up of copper-alloy scales backed onto leather, with a pull tie around the top. The gorget was open at the back were it fastened. A second example comes from a second century AD Thracian burial at Catalka in Bulgaria. The Catalka gorget consists of a thick iron ring; 0.162m diameter, and 0.07m high; made in two sections, with the sections being connected by a belt or strap. The outer surface was red in colour and the gorget appears to have been attached to the body of the mail shirt (**fig 16**).

In terms of use, the gorget was in the same class of armour as the greaves and *manicae* (segmental limb defences) namely it was battlefield wear for the close-order infantryman. Again like the other armour accessories it would otherwise probably have only been worn during training and full dress parades.

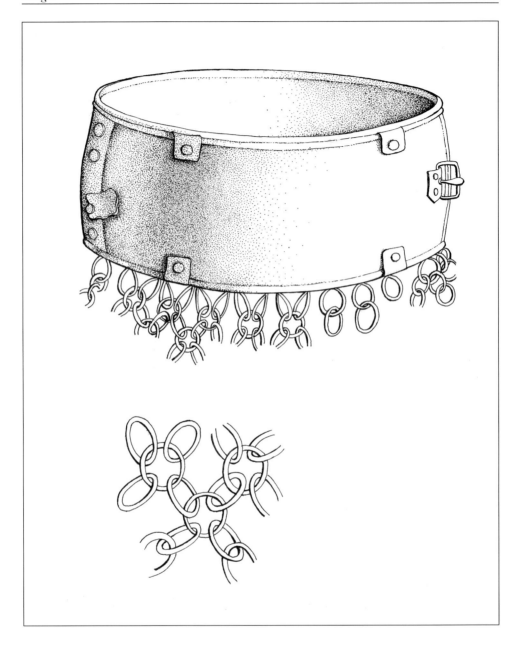

16   *The gorget from Catalka, Bulgaria, including a detail of the mail.*

(Redrawn by M. Daniels from Bujukliev 1986)

9 Manicae

BLACK KNIGHT
'Tis just a scratch.

ARTHUR
A scratch? Your arm's off.

Monty Python and The Holy Grail. 1977

Manicae, or segmental limb defences were first introduced into the Roman Army in the first century AD. Designed to protect the vulnerable, unarmoured, right (weapons) arm, the left arm being protected by the shield, there were probably first used in any number during Trajan's Dacian campaigns. Indeed, they are most famously represented on the Adamklissi metopes. However, depictions and finds from other parts of the Empire, notably Mainz and Newstead, point to a wider use than the Dacian Wars.

In the third century, although only attested on a late second/early third century sculpture from Alba Iulia, continuance of use throughout the whole of the period is highly probable, for a number of reasons. Despite the move towards greater levels of armour by both legionary and auxiliary units, both short sleeved (mail) and sleeveless (scale and *lorica segmentata*) armour was still used. Thus the purpose for which the *manicae* were designed (the protection of the right arm) still existed. Its continued use was also not in contradiction with the trend (of more armour) of the period. Indeed the move of the heavy infantryman away from 'fire and shock' and back to phalanx, made limb armour, be it long sleeved (mail or scale) or additional armour (*manicae*) more necessary. Finally the depiction of segmental limb armour in the *Notitia Dignitatum*, provides evidence for their use in the late Empire, thus allowing us to postulate continuance of use throughout the third century.

However, a caveat must be added, concerning their use. *Manicae* were not day-to-day wear but were designed to be worn by troops, legionary or auxiliary, acting as heavy infantry in either a pitched battle or a siege.

10 Composite armour

Tut! I have the best armour of the world: would it were day!

Shakespeare, *Henry V*, Act 3 Scene 7

Composite armour, namely where the cuirass was made up of more than one type of armour, is not a form of armour commonly associated with the Roman Army, being seen more as both an Oriental and Late Medieval style of armour. Indeed, if anything, the Roman Army is seen as being rather standardised in terms of its equipment, especially its armour. This view, however, is rather misleading and we would probably be closer to the truth envisaging a scenario where — as long as the Roman soldier had fully functional armour — then the Army did not mind what type it was. As long as it did the job it was required to do and was well maintained, then the type was a secondary consideration. If, however, the soldier did not have a well maintained set of armour (again type of armour being irrelevant) then only the failure on the soldier's part would count when punishment was awarded.

Having accepted the possibility of composite armour the next stage is to examine the evidence for it. The majority of which is representational, the one piece which is not, a fragment of *lorica plumata* (?) (scale with a mail backing) in Augsburg Museum, is unfortunately first century in date and therefore does not aid our understanding of composite armour in the third century as it is not known if this form continued in use into the third century.

Turning to the representational evidence, the relief from Arlon, France, which purports to show mail shirts with *segmentata* shoulder protection, is unfortunately for our purposes again first century and also in all probability does not depict composite armour. It more likely shows the far more common practice of shoulder doubling, which can be attested on both mail and scale shirts from the Republican period through to the second century AD.

The remaining representational evidence is, however, all datable to the late second or third centuries AD, and comprises a statue of a legionary (?) from Alba Iulia (late second/early third century), the grafitto of a *clibanarius* (?)(a heavily armoured cavalryman) from Dura Europos (third-century) and the tombstone of

17　*The composite armour (?) depicted on the tombstone of Severius Acceptus of* legio VIII Augusta, *Istanbul.*

(Redrawn by K.R. Dixon 1990)

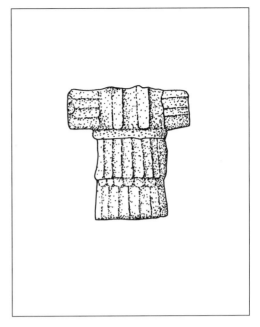

Severius Acceptus, Istanbul (third century). Of these the tombstone of Severius Acceptus is the most unpromising, as it probably depicts a *subarmalis* with *pteruges* (**fig 17**).

The remaining two, from Alba Iulia and Dura Europos, do however, in all likelihood depict composite armour. The first shows a set of armour made up from a *lorica segmentata* body with scale shoulders; whilst the second, from Dura Europos, depicts a set of armour with mail or scale on the chest and shoulders, vertical splints to the waist and a mail or scale skirt.

Thus although there is not a great deal of evidence, composite armour does appear to have been a feature of the Roman Army in the third century.

11 Shafted weapons

As Odeus was turning, the spear was fixed in the middle of his back between the shoulders and then driven on through the chest. He fell with a thud and his armour clattered about him.

Homer, *Iliad*, 5

Roman infantry in the third century armed with shafted weapons (which the majority were, archers being the exception) used either the *pilum*, or the javelin, or a combination of spear and javelin (**colour plates 7 & 8**).

In terms of construction the *pilum* and spear were made up of head, shaft and butt-spike; and the javelin of head and shaft (**fig 18**). *Pila*, of both the tanged and socketed variety, continued in use in this period. Depictions of *pila* on tombstones also show the continued use of bulbous weights, similar to those depicted on the Cancelleria Reliefs, Rome, and Adamklissi metopes, Romania. These weights occur either singly or in pairs, and although they would decrease the range of the *pilum* the extra weight would increase its penetrative power. None, however, survive in the archaeological record and thus it is not known if they were made of either metal or wood. Either is possible, with metal (lead?) being the more plausible, as it would then allow these bulbous additions to actually function as a weight; if they were wooden then any increase in weight would be minimal.

Spears and javelins in the main had what are today loosely termed 'leaf-shaped' spearheads (**colour plates 19 & 21**). There exists no accepted typology of 'leaf-shaped' spearheads for the Roman period. Indeed any such typology would be artificial as the Roman Army itself, in all probability, did not possess such a thing as a pattern book. Spearheads were most likely produced in generalised sizes and shapes. Small heads for javelins, large heads for thrusting spears, with those which where somewhere in-between, in terms of size, being used for either purpose. Thus the term 'leaf-shaped' although vague, does at least cover the whole gamut of shapes and provide a usable descriptive device.

Also used was a long thin spearhead with a solid triangular or square-sectional head. Originally introduced in the second century they continued in use into the third.

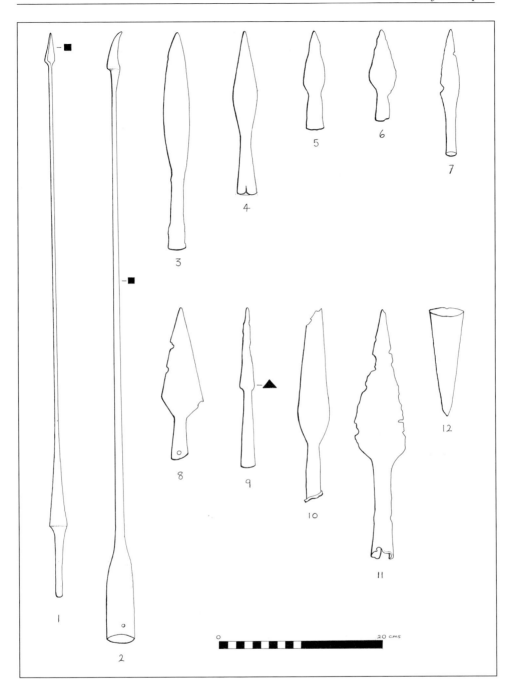

18   *Third-century spearheads and a butt spike. 1-2: Saalburg, 3: Buch, 4: Kunzing,*
      5-7: Saalburg, 8: Osterbrucken, 9: Kunzing, 10: Osterbrucken, 11: Saalburg,
      12: Osterbrucken.

      (Redrawn by M. Daniels from Bishop and Coulston 1993)

The butt-spike was literally a metal spike attached to the butt end of spears (**colour plate 20**), and also it would appear, from representations on tombstones, *pila*. There is no evidence for the employment of the butt-spike on javelins, and as will be seen such employment would have been without purpose.

In terms of manufacture the various types of spearhead were all made from iron which was left unhardened. The unhardening was probably deliberate as it would not only reduce production time, but would also allow for on-the-spot field repairs to be carried out by the soldier, without recourse to specialist facilities.

The types of wood used for the shafts of *pila*, spears and javelins varied and was to a large extent dependent upon localised supply. Ash was the preferred wood; however, hazel, willow, poplar and alder were also used. Coppicing was the preferred and undoubtedly main source of wood for spear and javelin shafts, although milled timber may also have at times been used. *Pila* shafts in the past had required working. However, the types of tangs and sockets employed on *pila* in the third century no longer required this, and thus *pila* used the same types of shafts as spears.

The question of spear length is problematic. There are no surviving complete examples from within the Empire and we are thus forced, in the main, to rely upon the literary and representational evidence. All three types of shafted weapon, *pilum*, spear and javelin are represented on the military tombstones of the period. The tombstone of Aurelius Mucianus, Apamea, Syria, shows the deceased clutching five javelins; Aurelius Lucianus, Rome, is holding a *pilum* in his left hand; and the tombstone Aprilius Spicatus, Istanbul, as well as the tombstones of unknown soldiers from Brigetio and Istanbul, all show the deceased holding a single spear. A non-funerary representation also exists; the troops on the 'Exodus' fresco, Dura Europos, are all armed with spears. Yet despite all of this, most of the representations cannot be said to give an accurate picture of the spear in respect to its length.

The spears on the 'Exodus' fresco are simple in the extreme and only show the top of the spear. The Brigetio and Istanbul tombstones confirm the use of a thrusting spear; however, these spears conveniently fit the available space, being no higher than the figure. Also the reduction in the size of the shield, on the tombstones of Aprilius Spicatus and on the example from Brigetio, in order to show more of the actual deceased, casts doubt on the accuracy, in terms of size, of the equipment portrayed. The tombstone of Aurelius Mucianus also precludes straightforward interpretation. The crude execution and small shield tend to militate against this being a perfectly accurate depiction of the deceased's equipment and indeed the shield is probably inaccurate. Further complicating the interpretation is the inscription on the tombstone, which describes Aurelius Mucianus as a 'trainee javelineer'. However, the five javelins depicted do fit Polybius's description of the thickness of a javelin (Polybius VI.22), they are, however, longer than the descriptions given by both Polybius and Vegetius. He may thus not be a close-order infantryman but he may rather be a skirmisher/light infantryman, and although both types of troops were armed with javelins, shaft length may well have varied.

The tombstone of Aurelius Lucianus, Rome, although incomplete, is probably accurate in its depiction of the shaft length of a *pilum*. In that the shaft depicted is approximately shoulder height, from the ground, which tallies with the literary descriptions of the weapon.

Of the three types of shafted weapons used by the Army in the third century, the literary evidence provides details of shaft length for two of the three, and vague generalities for the third. Unfortunately it is the thrusting spear which is only vaguely described. Although all of the sources agree that it was 'long', 'long' is very subjective term and open to a wide degree of latitude in its interpretation. For the *pilum* and the javelin, although we lack contemporary third-century descriptions, the detail provided by both Polybius and Vegetius in all probability mirrors the reality of the third century. Polybius states that the *pilum* (VI.23) had a shaft 3 cubits (1 cubit = 18-22in) in length, and that the javelin (VI.22) had a shaft the thickness of a finger and was 2 cubits in length. According to Vegetius the shaft of the *pilum* (II.15) was 5½ Roman ft (5 ft/162.8cm) long and that of the javelin (II.15) was 3½ Roman ft (3.4 ft/103cm) long.

As to the archaeological record, there are no complete surviving shafts from within the Empire. Wood survival does occur, but only in small quantities and it is only useful in determining the method of attachment and the species used. However, the contemporaneous third-century bog deposit at Illerup, Denmark, does contain a number of complete shafted weapons. In all cases the shafts are broken and in a large number of cases they are mixed up and thus no definite length can be safely calculated. However, in three cases the length of the shaft is measurable with a reasonable degree of confidence in terms of its accuracy. The three cases are all thrusting spears so it is thus possible to begin to tentatively put a figure to the subjective literary 'long'. The spear shaft lengths, not including spearhead, are 274cm, 256cm and 223cm (approximately 7-9ft). This is longer than is usually deemed the norm for the Roman infantryman, but is comparable with the 8ft long spears used by the Classical Greek Hoplite, and is thus probably correct (**colour plate 13**).

One feature of shafted weapons which is rarely considered is the subject of shaft decoration. Yet it is likely that such weapons were decorated by the soldier, although whether the decoration was unit specific or down to individual preference is unknown.

A *pilum* on the tombstone of a *beneficiarius* at Apamea has ribbons attached to the lower weight and the lines on the *pilum* held by Aurelius Lucianus may well delineate decorative bands of colour. The later *Notitia Dignitatum* and Ravenna mosaics also depict decorated spear shafts (**colour plates 7 & 8**). The *Notitia Dignitatum* contains illustrations of spears decorated with a 'candy stick/barber pole' pattern, whilst the Ravenna mosaics show soldiers holding spears decorated with horizontal bands of colour, whilst more contemporaneous Danish bog deposits contain the remains of spear shafts which were decorated with intricately carved interlace patterns, just below the socket of the spearhead (**fig 19**).

The distribution of shafted weapons within the Army was to some extent

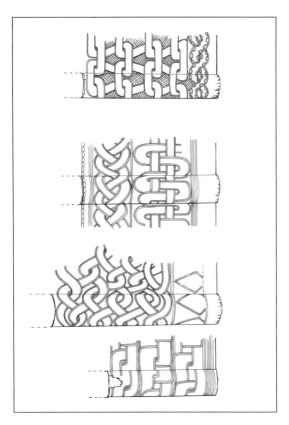

19   *Spearcraft decoration from Kragehul, Denmark.*

(Redrawn by M. Daniels from Engelhardt 1867)

determined by weapon type. However, the primary shafted weapon for the majority of the Imperial Roman Army, both legionary and auxiliary alike in the third century, was the thrusting spear. The *pilum* remained in use with some legionary and praetorian units, but its pre-eminence had passed. The javelin was used both in conjunction with the spear, giving the infantryman a short range missile capability; and on its own by light/skirmish troops, for whom the javelin was their primary weapon.

Shafted weapons divided neatly, in theory, into two distinct groups, namely missile weapons and thrusting weapons. However, in actuality the distinction is not so clear cut; Arrian's *Ektaxis kat' Alanon* (16) contains a description of the *pilum* as thrusting spear; and in the archaeological record, there is a substantial grey area of spearhead size, where it cannot be said with any degree of certainty whether the heads were for javelins or spears. It must also be borne in mind that *in extremis* the longest spear could be thrown and the smallest javelin could have been thrust into an enemy.

Unfortunately, there are no contemporary descriptions of either the javelin or the *pilum* in use which give details of the effective range and/or penetrative power of these weapons. All of the information on this subject is based upon comparative example and modern reconstruction. Experiments have shown that the *pilum* has a range of approximately 30m and can penetrate 30mm of pine or 20mm of ply at a range of 5m. Similar experiments conducted with reconstructed javelins have shown that they have a range of approximately 20m and can penetrate 18mm of oak at a range of 10m.

These ranges may not seem very great, however, it must be remembered that effective range was more important than maximum range. Indeed the Zulus, to draw a comparison, although capable of distance throwing realised that the javelin's effectiveness was dictated by range. They therefore tended to throw the javelin no further than 30yds (approximately 27.5m), for beyond this the force and accuracy of the weapon was greatly reduced. Whereas at 30yds or less they could be thrown both with great accuracy and also with sufficient force to transfix a human torso.

In terms of throwing rate, the picture is relatively simple for the *pilum*, but not so clear cut for the javelin. The *pilum* armed legionary would have acted the same in the third century as in previous centuries; namely a single volley at close range followed by a charge with swords drawn. Whereas the *pilum* was used predominantly as a volley weapon, the same was not true of the javelin. The javelin was used by close-order infantry, both legionary and auxiliary, to give them a secondary missile capability; it was also used by light infantry in both a skirmishing and support role. The numbers carried would also have varied depending upon troop type. Close-order infantry would probably have carried between two (the number shown carried behind a shield on a first-century relief from Mainz, Germany) and four (the maximum number carried by Zulu close-order infantry and also the maximum number, which experiments by The Arbeia Society have shown, that can be comfortably carried behind the shield).

Light troops, for whom the javelin was their primary weapon, would have carried far more, although how many more is unknown. The tombstone of Aurelius Mucianus, 'trainee javelineer', shows the deceased holding five javelins. They should be viewed more as a representation of his role, with the five javelins symbolising a bundle, rather than the actual number carried in battle.

Throwing rate for the javelin was thus not as clear cut as for the *pilum*. Some measure of what was achievable, in terms of throwing rate, can be seen in the results of an experiment by The Arbeia Society. They found that a man armed with five javelins, when charged by an 'enemy' 20m away, could loose all of his javelins in the time it took the running man to cross just over half the distance. This gave the 'javelineer' enough time to prepare either to receive the attack or to counter-charge, or to withdraw.

The armour-piercing capability of the *pilum* made it an effective missile weapon, deadly to both armoured and unarmoured opponents alike. Indeed a *pila* volley delivered at close range, less than 20m, could be devastating, not only in terms of the casualties inflicted but also by its ability to shake the morale of an attacking force, potentially fatally. The javelin, although not armour-piercing, was still seen as very effective against unarmoured opponents (Herodian VI.7.8), and was also in all probability effective against armoured opponents at extreme close range, 10m or less. The main advantage the Roman Army possessed in its use of javelins, over that of its barbarian adversaries, was its ability to deploy the weapon in extremely large numbers.

The effectiveness of the javelin and *pilum*, indeed of any missile weapon, in terms of numbers of casualties per javelins thrown or rounds fired is difficult to quantify, not least because of the lack of reliable data. There is, however, a single reference in the literature of the third century, which provides precisely this type of information namely number of javelin throws per kill. Julius Africanus (*Kestoi*. Fragments.1.1.80-81) writing in the early third century complains of poor marksmanship on the part of the Roman Army as they were only able to achieve one kill per ten javelins thrown. This is, however, to misunderstand the purpose of the javelin; it was not specifically a marksman's weapon, but was designed to be used *en mass* on the battlefield. To some extent it can be seen as a doctrine of firepower, with weight of numbers not only causing casualties but also having a detrimental effect on the enemy's morale.

The drawing of comparisons with late periods is problematic, especially in this field. The picture is complicated by the fact that the best data is available post-1815 when the phenomenon of the empty battlefield has further complicated the matter. However, at the battle of Maida, 4 July 1806, Kempt's Light Brigade fired a total of 3,780 rounds, in three volleys, and inflicted 430 casualties, an average of 8.7 rounds per hit. Thus, the one kill per ten javelins maybe seen as a more respectable achievement than Julius Africanus would have us believe.

The end of the second century saw a sea change in the role of the Roman infantryman. Prior to this period he had been primarily a swordsman; from this point on, however, he was a spearman. Indeed, according to Herodian (IV.10.3), an invincible one. His primary weapon, as has already been described, was a 7-9 ft long thrusting spear, held in the right hand and used in one of two ways, either overarm or underarm (**fig 20**).

The former method has the benefit of being artistically well represented, particularly on cavalry tombstones. More pertinently, it is employed by infantry on both the Arch of Constantine, Rome, and on a mosaic from the Piazza Armerina Villa, Sicily. However, these depictions more probably show the spear as javelin; for the infantry on the Arch of Constantine are at the bottom of a wall attacking the men on top of it, and the figure on the Piazza Armerina mosaic is taking part in a hunt and is in all probability throwing his spear at his prey rather than trying to stab it.

Depictions of the underarm use of the spear are less common. It appears on Shield II/the Amazon shield, from Dura Europos, where it is used by Greek warriors in combat with mounted Amazons. It is also employed, on one of the Adamklissi metopes (XXXI), by a legionary attacking a Dacian archer who is hiding (?) in the branches of a tree.

Detailed descriptions of the use of the spear in the literature of the period are unfortunately non-existent. This lack of literary description, combined with the debatable nature of the representational evidence, namely the paucity of the underarm depictions and the ambiguous nature of the overarm examples, allow

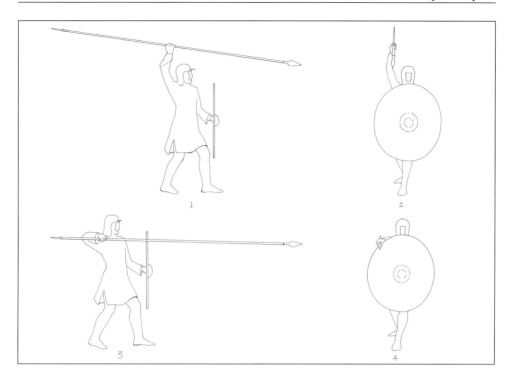

20　*A reconstruction illustrating the overarm and underarm use of the spear.*
　1: the overarm method from the side, 2: the overarm method from the front
　3: the underarm method from the side, 4: the underarm method from the front.
　(Drawn by M. Daniels)

no firm conclusions to be drawn from the contemporary sources with regard to the use of the spear.

How then was the spear used? Comparing the two methods there are a number of inherent drawbacks in the overarm use of the spear when compared to the underarm method. The spear, if it is to be used effectively must be stable; if it is stable then it can be controlled; if it is controlled then it can be used to lethal effect. With a 7-9ft long thrusting spear, this degree of control can only be achieved, in the overarm position, by holding the spear at or near the mid-point of the shaft. This however reduces the effective length of the spear to little more than the reach of a sword. In the underarm position, however, length was not sacrificed in order to achieve control. Indeed, the underarm method allowed the spear to be held quite close to the butt end and still be used effectively. A further drawback with the overarm use of the spear, was that it exposed the whole of the right arm (the weapons arm) to attack. Any attempt to use the shield to protect this vulnerable area would be counter productive, as it would either lead to the exposure of the lower body, or the impeding of the spear, or both. Finally a blow can be delivered with far greater force if the spear was held in the underarm as opposed to the overarm position. To draw a comparison, the Zulus found the overarm method to be a very ineffective way of using a spear, and indeed would jeer at any who used it. The underarm method, however, was passed on from generation to generation as the most effective way of using a spear, as it gave the warrior the ability to inflict devastating, incapacitating blows.

As a weapon of war the spear was very effective. Used underarm it not only gave the user a reach which far exceeded that of any hand-held weapon, but it could also, if sufficient force were applied, pierce shield and armour. However, the primary target area for the spearman was the face, which was neither armoured nor shielded. Secondary target areas were the throat, right arm and armpit, and the left shin. Of these areas only hits to the face, throat and armpit are potentially fatal. The importance of all these areas primary and secondary alike, lies not in the fact that a blow to one of these areas will kill, the first hit or hits can be merely crippling. Rather, they are important because in the main they are exposed, poorly armoured or shielded, and if hit with either sufficient force or sufficient regularity will cause either incapacitation for the rest of the battle or more importantly cause the victim to drop his shield. For although the spear could pierce the shield, there was no guarantee that it would; or that if it did, that it would retain enough force to wound. It was therefore preferable to remove the shield from the equation. The chest and abdomen would now be exposed to a series of killing blows. It was usual, indeed it was expedient, to deliver more than one blow, for the first may not have been fatal and even if it were there was no way of knowing. Blows would thus have been landed until the opponent fell, and thus ceased to be a threat.

The main drawback of the spear was the inherent weakness of the wooden shaft. The shaft could break or shatter against shield or armour, be cut by sword or become stuck in an opponent and break upon withdrawal. This flaw or failure in the spear had long been recognised, and a solution, the butt-spike found. Thus the loss of the spearhead, by whatever means, did not render the spear unusable.

The butt-spike had two main functions, both offensive. It was designed to act as a secondary spearhead should the main spearhead be broken off in battle, and it was used to deliver the *coup de grace* to any enemies lying on the field of battle, during the course of a battle. The first function involved the butt-spike being used as a normal spear, whereas in the second instance the spear would have been held vertically and the blow delivered by bringing the point of the butt-spike straight down. This would have been done to both the living and the already dead, as from the soldier's point of view 'you could never be too careful'. The butt-spike's stout design and small diameter made it an effective and efficient weapon, which was quite capable of piercing armour.

The butt-spike also had two further functions, both of which although secondary to its main functions, were still useful. It allowed the spear to be stood up when not in use, this was particularly important in battle when the soldier was throwing javelins; and, less importantly, it protected the base of the shaft against rot, wear and tear.

12 Swords

The majority of the spears shattered and they then engaged each other with swords.

Diodorus Siculus, *Universal History*, 15.86.2

The archaeological and representational evidence combine to show that the sword underwent a number of physical changes in the late second/early third centuries, the majority of which were purely cosmetic. The single, physical change that was not a mere question of fashion, concerned the sword itself, for the actual type of sword used by the Army changed.

To state briefly these changes; firstly, and most importantly, the short 'Pompeii' type (or *gladius* as it is more commonly known) ceased to be used and was replaced by the *spatha* for all categories of troops. Secondly, the sword was universally carried on the left-hand side and was suspended by a broad baldric, rather than the sword (waist) belt of earlier centuries. Thirdly, the scabbard-slide entirely replaced ring-suspension (**colour plates 5 & 6**).

The sword blades of the period have been divided into two categories; the 'Straubing/Nydam' type and the 'Lauriacum/Hromowka' type; although there is, obviously, a degree of overlap. The 'Straubing/Nydam' type had long, narrow slightly tapering blades; and a blade length to width ratio of 15-17:1. In actual terms blade lengths were 65-80cm (26-31in), whilst maximum blade width was 4.4cm ($1\frac{3}{4}$in). The 'Lauriacum/Hromowka' type was shorter and wider, with a parallel edged blade and a triangular point. The blade length to width ratio was 8-12:1, whilst actual blade lengths were 55.7-65.5cm (22-26in) and blade widths fell within the range of 6.2-7.5cm ($2\frac{1}{2}$-3in) (**fig 21**).

In a departure from earlier constructional techniques, many third-century swords were pattern-welded. A number of swords also had a groove(s) or fuller(s) running down their blades. The fuller was designed to give a deeper backing to the edge, without the need to either increase the weight of the blade or reduce the blade's flexibility. Some blades were decorated with an inlaid figure or figures. The inlay, in either *orichalcum* (an alloy of zinc and copper) or other contrasting metals, was at the hilt end of the blade, and took the form of either a god/goddess (Mars, Minerva or Victory) or a standard(s), an eagle or a wreath. These figures had their head downwards towards the point and were thus upside down when the sword was in its scabbard; however, when the sword was used they were the

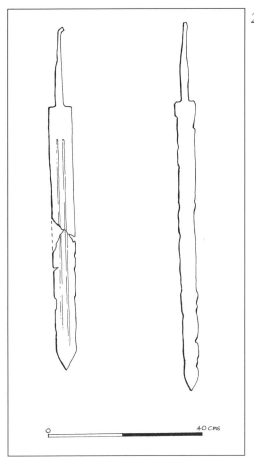

21   Third-century sword blades, both are from Augst, Switzerland.

(Redrawn by M. Daniels from Bishop and Coulston 1993)

4·0 cms

correct way up. Their purpose was undoubtedly twofold, they would have had a minor decorative function, but their main function would have been religious. They would have imbued the sword (and thus the swordsman) with the power of the god (goddess or guardian spirit) and given it/him the ability (providing the god have been suitably propitiated) to make every blow a killing blow (**figs 22 & 23**).

The hilt divided into three separate sections; the guard, the grip and the pommel (**fig 24**). The guards were semi-oval and rectangular, made of ivory, bone, or wood. Grips were made of ivory, bone or wood, and could be plain or decorated. Where decorated, this took the form of either ribbing, or spiral twists, or a basket-weave design. Pommels tended to be elliptical, and were made from either wood, ivory or bone. Metal hilt fittings tended to be confined to a washer on top of pommel through which the tang passed. The tang being then beaten into a knob in order to hold the washer and indeed the whole hilt assemblage in place. The sword could also have a metal guard plate, which completely covered the bottom of the guard, whilst in the case of a number of the Danish bog finds, the guard and pommel were decorated with metal nails. All of these forms are represented in both the archaeological and representational record. A further form

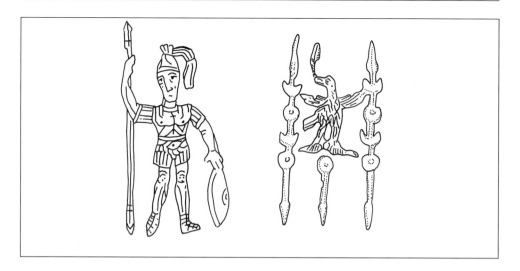

22 *Decorative sword inlays of Mars, and an eagle flanked by military standards, from South Shields, Great Britain.*

(Redrawn by K.R. Dixon from Rosenquist 1967-68)

absent archaeologically but represented on a number of tombstones and sarcophagi, and also depicted on Sassanid Persian depictions of Roman emperors, was the eagle-headed pommel. In the majority of depictions, the beak points along the grip. However, on the Sassanid reliefs the beak is at a right angle to the grip, very like the statue of the Tetrarchs in St. Mark's Square, Venice.

Scabbards in the main do not tend to survive, although fragments have been found at Dura Europos and in some of the Danish bog deposits. The surviving examples were either plain wood or wood covered with leather. The exception being a particularly fine example from Khisfine, Syria, which was made entirely (scabbard, chape, and slide and for that matter the whole hilt assemblage) from ivory (**colour plate 11**).

The chape was designed to provide a decorative, protective end to the scabbard. Made from, bone, ivory, copper-alloy, and iron they could be plain or decorated. Decoration could take the form of engraving, or inlaying (surviving iron examples are inlaid with either niello or contrasting metals), or a single gold rivet through the centre of the chape (as in the Khisfine example). As to form, peltate and heart-shaped chapes continued in use throughout the Empire in the third century. Alongside these older forms, two new types, the box chape and the circular chape, were introduced. The box chape, as a form, appears to have been limited to Europe and, does not appear in the representational record (**colour plates 17 & 18**). Of all the forms of chape used in the third century, the type most commonly represented in the art of the period was the circular chape. They occur most often on tombstones, but also appear on reliefs and mosaics. They appear to have been commonly used throughout the Empire, with the exception of Britain where their

23 *A decorative sword inlay of the goddess Victory, from Ovre Stadu, Norway.*

(Redrawn by K. R. Dixon from Rosenquist 1967-68)

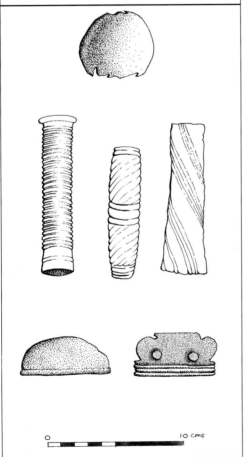

24 *Grip assemblages.*
Top: a pommel from Zugmantel
Middle: grips from (l-r) Cannstatt, Buch, Zugmantel
Bottom: guards from (l-r) Butzbach, Niederbieber.

(Redrawn by M. Daniels from Bishop and Coulston 1993)

1   *Unarmoured infantryman*
    (Painting by M. Daniels)

2 Thoracomachus
(Painting by M. Daniels)

3 Armoured infantryman   Mail 1
(Painting by M. Daniels)

4   *Armoured infantryman   Scale 1*
   (Painting by M. Daniels)

5 *Armoured infantryman   Mail 2*
   (Painting by M. Daniels)

6 *Armoured infantryman   Scale 2*
  (Painting by M. Daniels)

7 *Armoured infantryman   Mail 3*
   (Painting by M. Daniels)

8 *Armoured infantryman   Scale 3*
   (Painting by M. Daniels)

9 Armoured infantryman Mail 4
(Painting by M. Daniels)

10 *Libyan Hide*
   (Painting by M. Daniels)

11   *Foot Archer*
      (Painting by M. Daniels)

12   *Fighting stance as seen from the front*
      (Painting by M. Daniels)

13   *Fighting stance as seen from the side*
      (Painting by M. Daniels)

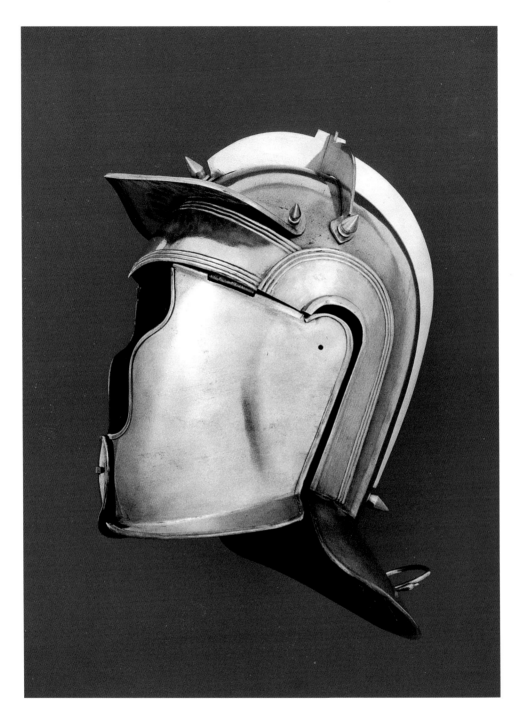

14   *A reconstruction of the Heddernheim helmet*
     (Photograph courtesy of the Museum of the University and the Society of Antiquaries
     of Newcastle upon Tyne)

15 (left)   A reconstruction of a dolphin scabbard-slide from Corbridge, Great Britain
16 (right) A reconstruction of the Carlisle eagle Phalera
         (Photographs by I.P. Stephenson)

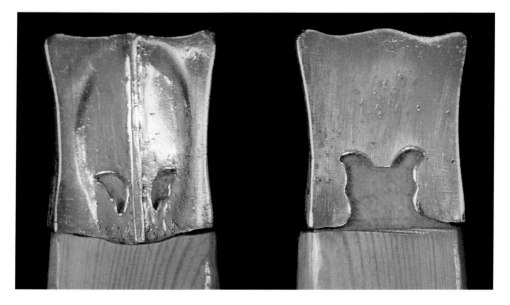

17 & 18   A reconstruction of a box chape from Corbridge — front (left) and back (right)
         (Photograph by I.P. Stephenson)

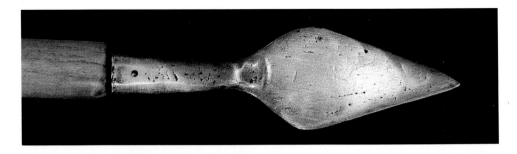

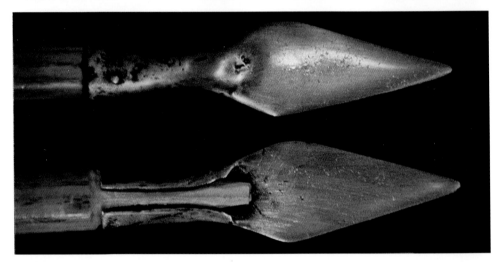

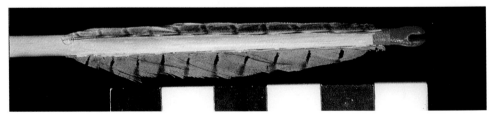

19   *A reconstruction of a leaf-bladed spearhead*
20   *A reconstruction of a butt-spike*
21   *Reconstructed leaf-bladed javelin heads*
22   *A reconstruction showing the tail end of an arrow*
      (Photographs by I.P. Stephenson)

25 *A detail of the tombstone of Aprilius Spicatus, Istanbul. Of particular note is the circular chape.*

(Drawn by K. R. Dixon)

virtual absence may well be attributable to regional fashion (**figs 25, 26 & 27**).

The late second/early third century saw the introduction of the scabbard-slide as a replacement for ring suspension. Scabbard-slides were either cast copper-alloy or made from iron, ivory or bone. They were attached near to the top of what would have been the outer face of the scabbard. The iron and copper-alloy examples had two or three studs projecting from the bottom of the scabbard-slide. These studs would have been keyed into holes in the scabbard and glued in place, binding (of either cloth or leather) would then have been wrapped around both the scabbard and slide, further securing it in place. The ivory and bone examples lacked these projections, and were attached simply by glueing and binding.

Archaeologically, they are very common. They also came in a number of different forms. Bone and ivory examples could be flat and waisted, or raised and lobate. Copper-alloy pieces were cast with decorative ribs or fluting, and decorative terminals. The terminals could be heart-shaped, or foliate, or rings, or crescents, or peltate in form. Alternatively, the copper-alloy examples were elaborately cast as an elongated dolphin (**colour plate 15**). Iron examples tended, in the main, to be long, thin and triangular in plan, and if decorated then the decoration was on this upper face, and consisted of niello inlay. There is a single example of an iron dolphin scabbard-slide. It was found in a grave, at Stuttgart-Bad Cannstatt, Germany, and is in very poor condition (**figs 28, 29 & 30**).

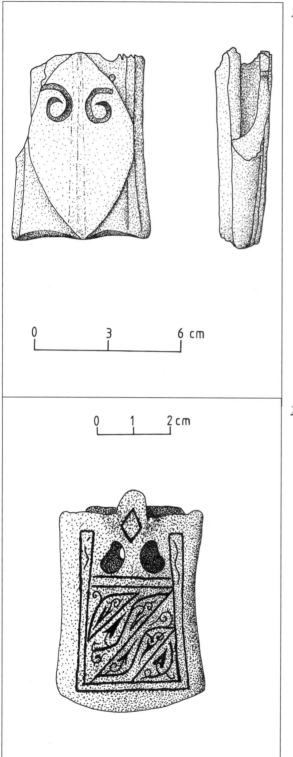

26 A third-century bone box chape from Niederbieber, Germany.

(Redrawn by K.R. Dixon from Oldertstein 1976)

27 A third-century iron box chape with niello decoration from Vimose, Denmark.

(Redrawn by K.R. Dixon from Engelhardt 1869)

28 *A copper-alloy dolphin scabbard-slide from Jagsthausen, Germany.*

  (Redrawn by K.R. Dixon from Koch 1971)

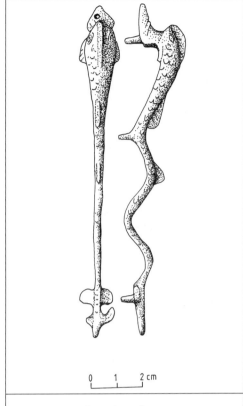

29 *An iron scabbard-slide with niello decoration from Vimose, Denmark.*

  (Redrawn by K.R. Dixon from Hundt 1959/60)

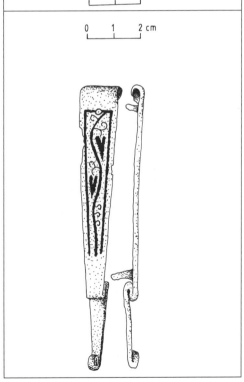

30   *A reconstruction showing the scabbard slide in situ.*

(Photograph by I.P. Stephenson)

The baldric is undoubtedly one of the best attested pieces of military equipment in the representational record, as it appears on practically all of the surviving military tombstones of the period, as well on a number of reliefs. It took the form of a broad belt, which always rested on the right shoulder and ran diagonally across the body, suspending the sword on the left-hand side. No examples survive from within the Empire, although, a number of contemporaneous examples survive. The best examples come from the bog deposits of Vimose, Denmark, and Thorsbjerg, Germany. The Thorsbjerg bog deposit yielded two examples, both incomplete. They were, respectively, 1.055m ($3\frac{1}{4}$ft) long by 9.1cm ($3\frac{1}{2}$in) wide; and 71cm (28in) long and 7cm ($2\frac{3}{4}$in) wide; both possessed two *phalerae*. Vimose also yielded to examples, one of which, was practically complete. The best preserved, most complete, example was 1.185m (4ft) long and 8cm (3in) wide. One end was cut off square, whilst the other tapered over a distance of 25cm (9in) to a width of 1.2cm ($\frac{1}{2}$in). The second example was incomplete, and measured 1.005m ($3\frac{1}{4}$ft) long by 8.6cm (3in) wide. Both possessed a single *phalera*, with the *phalera* on the complete example piercing the centre of the baldric 28.6cm (11in) from the wide, square end.

The baldric worked as a sword suspension method, by having the broad end with the *phalera* going across the front of the body. The tapering end went over the back, and the narrow end passed across the front of the scabbard, and through the scabbard-slide. It then wrapped around the scabbard went back through the scabbard-slide and finally fastened onto the eye on the back of the *phalera*. It was important that the second time it passed through the scabbard-slide that it was

31 An openwork phalera *from Egypt, depicting a suckling Romulus and Remus. The inscription reads LEG(IONIS) VI FERR (ATAE) F (IDELIS) C (ONSTANTIS) FEL (ICIS).*

(Drawn by K.R. Dixon)

higher up than the first time, because this tipped the hilt of the sword forwards, making it easier to grasp when drawing in battle. The baldric fastened to the eye of the *phalera* either by being tied, as was the case with one of the Vimose examples, or alternatively it would have passed through the eye of the *phalera* and been folded back on itself and sewn in place. The first method may have the benefit of archaeological evidence, however, experiment has shown the second to be more secure.

Baldric *phalerae* have been found on a number of sites, both within and outside, the Empire. They came in a variety of styles, both plain and decorated. The decoration took the form of concentric circles, perforated geometric patterns, raised radiating petals, or cast openwork designs. The openwork examples varied from the relatively simple (swastikas, radiating hearts, spokes, Celtic, and peltate designs), to the elaborate. Of all the elaborate designs, the most common, was of an eagle clutching thunderbolts, and encircled by an inscription which read OPTIME MAXIME CON[SERVA]; which translates as 'Best [and] greatest [referring to Jupiter] protect' (**colour plate 16**).

Decoration was not solely confined to the *phalera*, the baldric itself could also be decorated. At its simplest, the decoration took the form of a pattern stitched into the leather, the Vimose baldrics being decorated in this way with dolphin and foliate designs (**colour plate 11**). Perforated metal appliqués were also used, and indeed were illustrated on the military tombstones of the period. A number of rectangular plates and heart shaped copper-alloy baldric terminals have also been discovered, and these finds correspond to the ivy-leaf baldric terminals depicted on a number of tombstones. Although many are incomplete, their form has been established; they were made up of a rectangular plate, which attached to the baldric's broad end, and a heart shaped pendant, which was attached via a hinge to

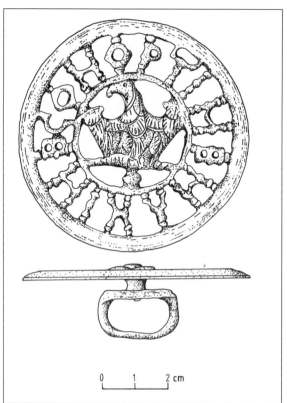

32   The Carlisle eagle phalera.

(Redrawn by K.R. Dixon from Allason-Jones 1985)

0   1   2 cm

the rectangular plate. A simple perforated example was found at Lyon, France, whilst a more elaborate cast openwork example was found at Silchester, Great Britain. The most elaborate examples were cast with inscriptions, and were designed to form a set with an eagle *phalera*. The complete inscription would have read OPTIME MAXIME CON[SERVA](*phalera*)/NUMERUM OMNIUM (rectangular plate)/MILITANTIUM(pendant). The message was designed as a good luck charm, imploring Jupiter's protection, and it translates as 'Best [and] greatest protect [us] a troop of fighting men all' (**figs 31-36**).

Change of sword type (the *spatha* was a slashing sword) naturally resulted in a change of use. However, the literature of the period points, rather obliquely, to another important change, that of status. Herodian (IV.10.3), narrating events during the reign of Antoninus (Caracalla) AD 211-17, describes the Roman infantryman as an invincible close-quarter spearman. The perceived invincibility of Roman infantry at close-quarters is nothing new, to a large extent, it is today and was then, taken for granted. During the Late Republic and Early Empire the Roman infantryman was primarily a swordsman. The late-second/early-third century, however, saw the Roman infantryman revert to the weapons (thrusting spear and slashing sword) and tactics of the Hoplite. The spear, thus, became the primary weapon, relegating the sword to a subsidiary role, both in combat and in literature.

33   Decorative, openwork baldric plates from Zugmantel, Germany.

(Redrawn by K.R. Dixon from Oldenstein 1976)

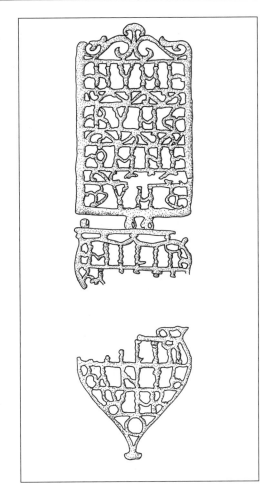

The move from a thrusting sword (the 'Pompeii' type), to a slashing sword (the *spatha*), necessitated a change in target areas for the infantryman during combat. The face, chest and abdomen became in the main the preserve of the spear. These areas were, however, not exclusively the preserve of the spear as the *spatha*, like the 'Mainz' and 'Pompeii' type swords of earlier centuries, was multifunctional. Although its ability to be used as a thrusting sword should be seen more as a secondary design feature. The emphasis was most definitely **cut** and thrust, as opposed to the earlier **thrust** and cut.

Before discussing the new target areas and in consequence the weapon's effectiveness, the first thing to consider is — how was a blow delivered?

The *Rules and Regulations for the Sword Exercise of the Cavalry,* issued by the Adjutant-General's Office, of the British Army, on 1 December 1796, required all blows to be delivered with the arm straight. This was in order to maximise the reach and protect the elbow (as a blow in that quarter immediately decides the contest in the enemy's favour). Although this may not seem immediately relevant, a number of similarities exist which allow this comparison a degree of validity.

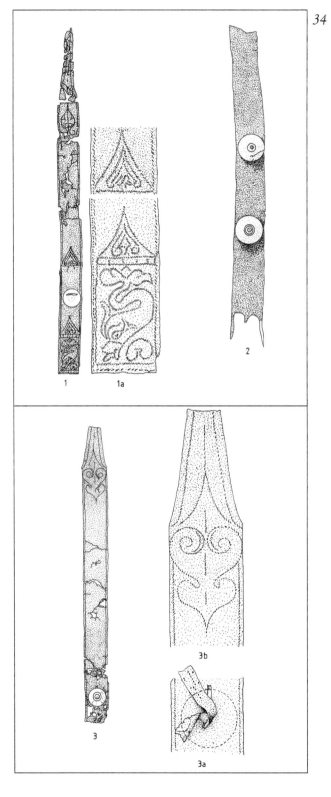

34 Leather baldrics from the Danish bog deposits. 1, 1a, 3, 3a, and 3b are from Vimose, whilst 2 is from Thorsbjerg.

(Redrawn by K.R. Dixon from Stjernquist 1954)

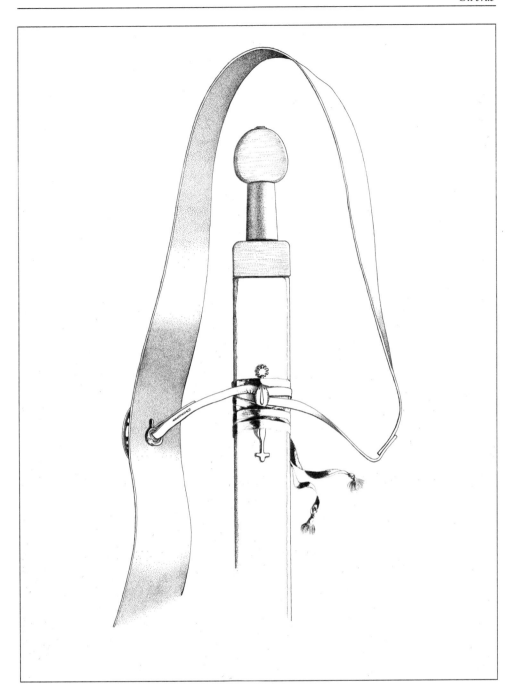

35   *Reconstruction of sword suspension — front.*

      (Drawn by M. Daniels)

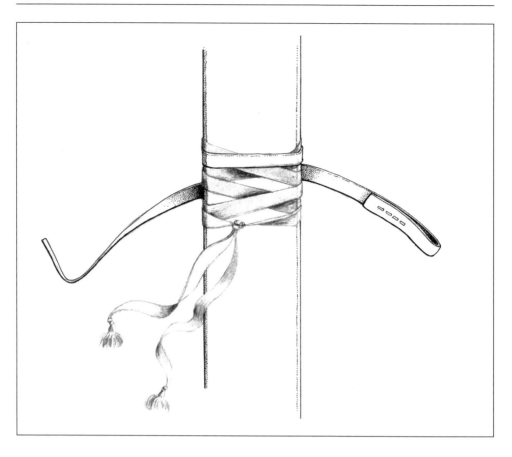

36   *Reconstruction of sword suspension — back.*

(Drawn by M. Daniels)

Firstly, weapon type: both types of soldier were armed with long, slashing swords. The killing zone, or faible, on such swords ran from approximately the mid-point (in terms of length), to the point, thus in both cases it made sense to maximise reach. Secondly, opponent height. In both cases, the weapons were used against opponents of equal height. Thirdly, the use of the whole arm allowed more force to be put into the blow than if were delivered solely from the elbow. Finally, blows to the elbow, irrespective of historical period, are crippling, and do, as has been stated above, decide the issue in the enemy's favour. Thus, it is likely that the third-century Roman kept his arm straight when swinging his sword.

The target areas, for an infantryman armed with a slashing sword such as the *spatha*, were the head, the shoulders (if visible), the right arm and the left leg. Blows would have been delivered diagonally downward right to left or left to right. The thrust was best used in pursuit where the length of the sword could be fully utilised. At close quarters if the point were given and parried, then the attacker's guard was in danger of being fatally compromised, as both his sword arm and armpit were open to counter attack. It was therefore safer to attack with the cut and pursue with the thrust, although, the spear, if intact, was far superior in the pursuit.

The *spatha* was not designed for finesse, but was designed to either hack a man to pieces or to beat him to a bloody pulp. Ammianus Marcellinus (XXXI.7.14) graphically describes its ability to split heads in two, whilst the seventh-century historian John of Antioch, in his *Fragmenta Historicorum Graecorum*, describes the effect of a practically identical weapon upon an unarmoured man. The blow, according to John of Antioch, struck the collarbone and pierced the body down to the hip.

On the battlefield, the *spatha* was used either when the spear was broken, lost, or when the lines were so close together as to make use of the spear dangerously impracticable. As with the spear the infantryman would have landed blows upon an opponent until he ceased to be perceived as a threat. Bodies found in the grave pits at Wisby (1361), Sweden, tended to have a number of minor wounds (blows to the arms and legs) and a serious blow (usually to the head) which undoubtedly proved fatal. Against armour, although the sword could penetrate an armoured opponent if sufficient force were put into the blow, in the main the blunt trauma/bloody pulp principle applied. Namely if you hit someone hard enough and often enough with an iron bar, they will break.

13 Military dagger

After Severus had given this order, the Illyrian troops rushed forward
and took away from the soldiers the daggers they were carrying, which
were inlaid with silver and gold.

Herodian, II.13.10

The military dagger, or *pugio*, of the Roman Army, used by legionary and auxiliary alike, continued in use into the third century. However, surviving examples, most notably from Kunzing, Germany (**fig 37**), where 51 blades and 29 sheaths were included in the iron horde found on the site, but also from other parts of the Empire, including Copthall Court in London (**colour plate 5**), show two distinct differences between third-century and earlier Imperial examples. Firstly, surviving third-century examples are plainer, both in terms of hilt and scabbard decoration, and secondly they are often larger than examples from earlier centuries.

Before looking at the military dagger in more detail let us first examine these two apparent dissimilarities with earlier periods (there is no evidence that the military dagger continued in use into the fourth century). Firstly, the question of plainness. Although the surviving examples lack the decorative rivet heads seen on the hilts of the military dagger of the first century and although scabbard decoration in the third century appears to have been confined to simple punched dots, it is worth remembering that Septimius Severus stripped the Preatorian Guard of their silver and gold inlaid daggers (Herodian II.13.10). Thus more decorative examples probably existed in the third century. However, as they have not as yet occurred in the archaeological record speculation as to the type of decoration used is fruitless.

In terms of size this is more a general as opposed to an absolute rule. For although third century military daggers are in the main larger, examples from the Principate show blade lengths the same as or in some cases even longer than third-century examples.

In specific terms two blade shapes and two hilt types were used in the third century. Despite this apparent symmetry there is, however, no correlation between blade shape and hilt type. The blade shapes were either parallel or waisted, with, in both cases, two central channels running the length of the blade and in the process defining a mid-rib. In terms of blade length, those found at Kunzing are approximately 28cm long, whilst the example from Copthall Court was 30cm long. Hilts were either 'T'-shaped with crescent pommels, or purely organic and thus lost to us.

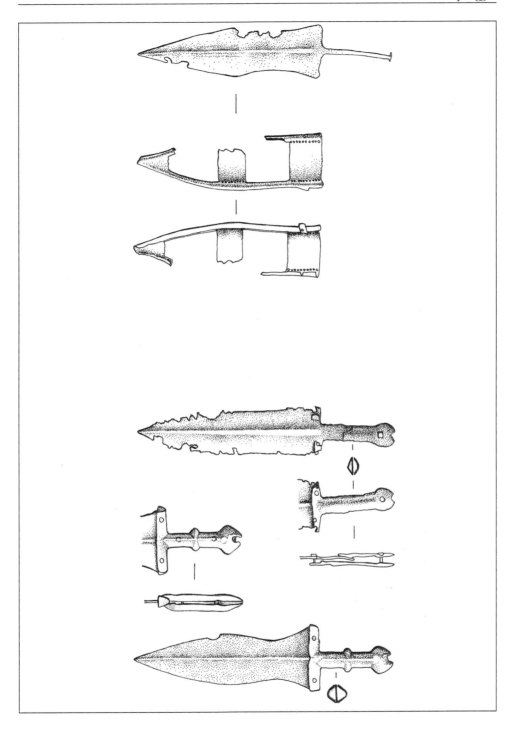

37   *Third-century military daggers and their scabbards from Kunzing, Germany.*

(Redrawn by M. Daniels from Herrmann 1969)

The iron sheaths, as can be seen in the illustrations, had simple punched decoration and only provided a front to the sheath, the majority of the sheath being in all probability made up from thin slats of wood covered in leather. The leather would show through, decoratively, onto the front of the scabbard in the panels defined by the edge guttering, chape, mid-plate and mouth of the scabbard.

The military dagger retained the now anachronistic ring suspension method, and had a pair of rings on either side of the scabbard, with two rings on the mouth plate and two on the mid-plate. Leather straps going through either the top or middle pair, presumably depending upon individual preference, would then have hung the dagger from either the waist belt or as a baldric over the left shoulder. This choice, of either waist belt or baldric, would again depend upon personal preference, except in the case of scale armour where a waist belt would not be practical and a baldric would have to be worn. In either case the weapon would have been suspended by the soldiers' right hand side ready for us.

As to that use, the military dagger should not be seen as a large over-ornate camping knife or machete. It was a weapon and although at times the Roman soldier may well have put it to some non-military uses, this should not detract from the items primary function.

In terms of use, the first questions to be asked are why was another weapon, on top of the spear, javelins, and long sword, required and why was that weapon a large dagger? Unfortunately the literary sources are silent on this matter and we must therefore rely on comparative evidence and conjecture.

The most apposite comparisons come from the medieval *cultellus* and from a work entitled the *Military Art of Training*, published in 1622. The Anglo-Saxon *seax*, which was in many ways a similar weapon to the military dagger, cannot, however, provide a point of comparison, for like the military dagger its role remains one of conjecture.

Turning to the *cultellus*, this was a large dagger in use from the eleventh to the fourteenth century. It was seen as being almost exclusively an infantry weapon, and was employed in two main circumstances. Firstly it was used to despatch unhorsed cavalry and secondly in close combat as a auxiliary to the sword. The *Military Art of Training* sees the dagger in a similar light, namely as a companion to the sword; however, it also stressed the dagger's advantage over the sword at close quarters and as a weapon for the dispatch of the wounded. It also stated that the dagger should be carried because of its handsome appearance, and indeed, style and fashion should never be disregarded when considering the function and appearance of military equipment.

Returning to the military dagger, the weapon does appear ideal for the rapid and certain dispatch of both the wounded and unhorsed enemy cavalrymen. In addition, in the confines of the breach, or in a mine it would make a more effective and efficient weapon then either the sword or spear, both of which require space to wield. On the battlefield, however, it must be seen as being ancillary to these weapons, although its use *in extremis* must not be ruled out.

14 Short swords

Those fighting before the standards, around the standards and in the front line
were called *principes*. This was the heavy armament which had helmets,
cataphracts, greaves, shields, large swords called *spathae*, and other smaller
swords called *semispathia*.

Vegetius, *Epitoma Rei Militaris*, II.15

Vegetius (II.15), writing in the fourth century, tells us that the Ancient Legionary
was armed with a long sword called a *spatha* and a shorter, smaller sword called a
semispatha, of which no positively identified examples exist.

However, finds of short swords (not, however, of the Pompeii type) from
Kunzing, Germany (**fig 38 & colour plate 6**), and Augst, Switzerland, dateable
to the third century, may indeed represent the *semispatha*. Unfortunately, there is
no way of saying definitely whether they are or are not Vegetius' *semispatha*. In
terms of the swords themselves, the best examples come from the Kunzing iron
horde, which contained 14 of these short swords.

The Kunzing swords were pattern-welded and had a size range of 37.2- 54.7cm
total length, and a blade length range of 23.1-38.9cm. The shape of the swords,
ranged from parallel, to slightly tapering, to fully triangular, when viewed face on.
Hilts do not survive, but were probably of the same design and material as those
used on the *spatha*. Scabbards, also, were most likely as per the *spatha* (rather than
the military dagger), with corresponding scabbard fittings, namely a scabbard slide
and chape. The actual suspension method could have been either a thin baldric
hung over the left shoulder, or alternatively the sword could have been suspended
from a waist belt. In either case the sword would have hung on the right side, and
would have been used instead of the military dagger. It would have fulfilled the
same tactical role as the military dagger, namely it would have been used in the
close-quarters of the breach and the mine and *in extremis* on the battlefield.

As to who would have used this type of sword, there is no reason to see it as
anything other than a standard piece of equipment for all ranks of the Roman
Army. The soldier, be he legionary or auxiliary, was probably expected to have, in
good working order, a long sword and an other short thrusting weapon, and the
Army probably did not care whether it was a military dagger or a short
sword/*semispatha*, as long as it worked.

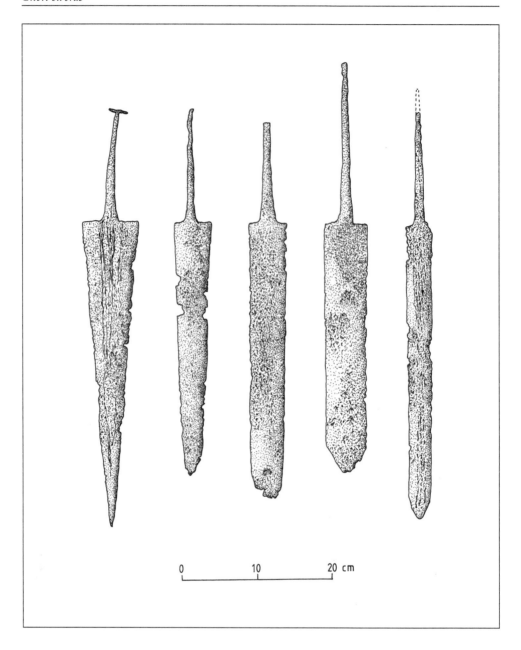

38 Short swords from the Kunzing iron hoard.

(Redrawn by K.R. Dixon from Herrmann 1969)

15 The bow and the sling

The torrent swept into them and hurled them down in whole companies.

G.W. Steevens, *With Kitchener to Khartoum*. 1898

Finds of ear- and grip-laths (the only surviving parts of the composite bow) (**fig 39**), from a number of military sites throughout the Empire, coupled with representations of the bow in both mosaics and sculptures from the Eastern part of the Empire, confirm the continued use of the composite bow by the Army in the third century (**fig 40 & colour plate 11**).

Vegetius (I.14) states that self-bows, ie. plain wooden bows, were used in training. This may well have been the case in the third century, however, such weapons were merely training weapons. Once sufficiently proficient the archer would then have moved onto the composite bow and used it for the remainder of his term of service. The composite bow, so named because it is constructed from a composite of wood, bone, horn and sinew, was used because the method of construction and the materials employed allowed the bow to impart a greater degree force to the arrow when fired, compared to a self-bow of the same draw weight (**fig 41**).

In terms of range, the above information on draw weights can only allow relative comparison to be made between the two types of bow. The actual range or performance of the composite bow is open to debate, and a number of varied figures have been suggested. Vegetius (II.23) recommended a practice range of 274m, while later Islamic works expected an archer to display consistent accuracy at 69m. Modern research tends to place effective range at between 50-150m, and maximum range at between 165-230m.

The reason for these discrepancies, and the mere 15m which separates the upper end of effective range from the lower end of maximum range, are the large number of externalities which must be accounted for when attempting to estimate the bow's performance. Unfortunately most of these variables remain conjecture. Range is as much dependant upon the man as the bow and coupled with this was bow quality — the better made the composite bow, the more tailored to the individual archer's height, draw weight and length, the better the performance. In

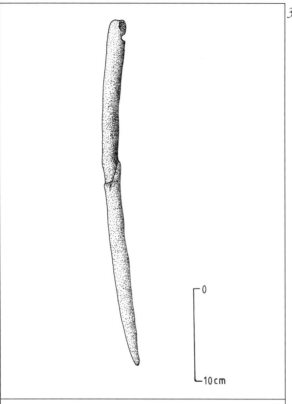

39 The ear-lath of a composite bow from Caerleon, Great Britain.

(Drawn by K.R. Dixon)

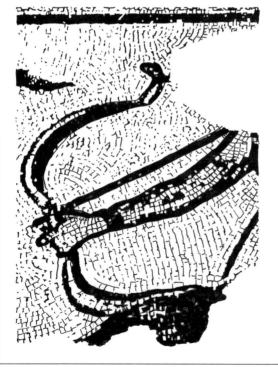

40 A detail of the Triclinos hunt mosaic from Apemae, Syria, showing the composite bow in use.

(Drawn by K.R. Dixon)

41   The basic shape of the composite bow when strung.

(Redrawn by J.R.A. Underwood from Coulston 1985)

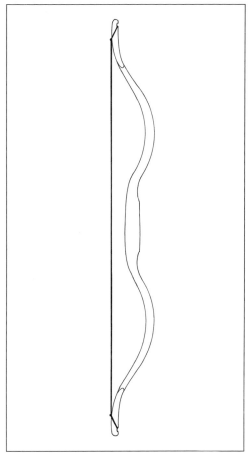

addition infantry bows would have been more powerful than cavalry bows, and this would again have effected the range.

Range is, however, only part of performance; accuracy and effectiveness must also be considered. Accuracy was governed by the target's size and rate of movement, as well as the skill of the individual archer. In actuality the archer would have practised shooting at a stationary target, and whilst this level of accuracy — the ability to pick-off individuals — would have been useful in the archer's role as a skirmisher (Herodian VII.2.2), the archer's main task was to stand behind his own infantry and shoot, indirectly, at a large enemy troop formation. In this case accuracy was more concerned with all of the arrows arriving on the target area or zone at the same time, than with individual marksmanship.

The second factor, effectiveness, was itself governed by two factors, namely the target's vulnerability and the type of arrowhead used. In the East and against the Sarmatians on the Danube, the Romans were presented with heavily armoured opponents, whereas in the West, Germanic warbands provided softer targets being in the main only protected by a shield. The types of arrowheads used by the

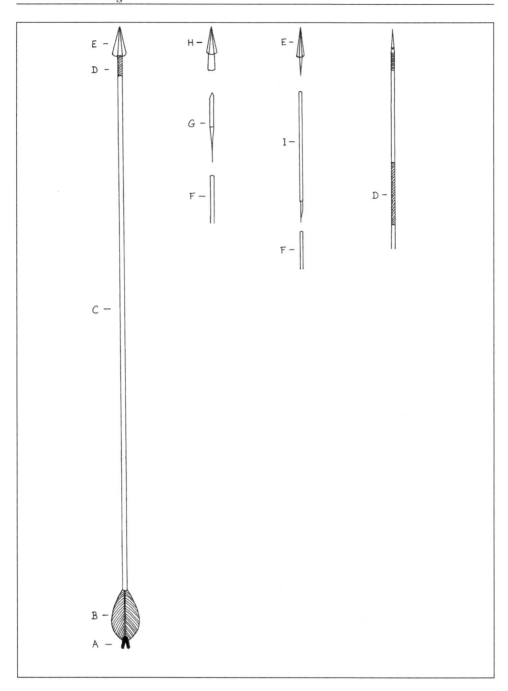

42   Arrow technology. A: Nock, B: Fletching, C: Stele, D: Sinew Binding,
     E: Head tanged, F: Reed stele, G: Wooden pile tanged, H: Head socketed,
     I: Wooden fore-shaft tanged.

     (Redrawn by M. Daniels from Coulston 1985)

43   *Third-century arrowheads from the*
      Saalburg, Germany.
      A: tanged trilobate,
      B: socketed bodkin.
      (Redrawn by K.R.Dixon from
      Jacobi 1897)

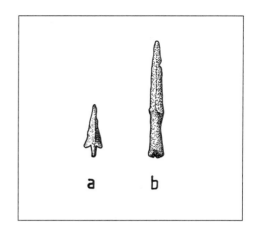

Roman Army in the third century reflected these different penetrative requirements. Bodkin heads (**colour plate 11**) were used for armour piercing, be it shield or body armour, whilst trilobate, triple-or quadruple-vaned were more effective against unarmoured horses and men.

In terms of arrow technology (**fig 42**) heads were either tanged or socketed (**fig 43**) and were glued and bound to the shafts (*stele*). The *stele* was made from either wood, reed or cane. Where reed or cane was used the head was first attached to a wooden pile, which was then glued onto the reed or cane *stele*. The piles reduced the risk of the reed splitting on impact, which would, if it occurred, reduce the arrow's penetrative power. The remains of the reed or cane arrows from Dura Europos show that the surface of the shaft was roughened and the fletching glued onto this roughened surface.

As to the method of release employed, the representational evidence shows the 'Mediterranean' release (where the fingers are used to draw the bow string) (**colour plate 22**) being used, whilst the *stele* from Dura Europos combined with the recent discovery of a thumb stall from Vindolanda, Great Britain, provide evidence for the use of the 'Mongolian' release (where the thumb is used to draw the bow string). There is no evidence pointing to a hard and fast rule concerning the method of release employed by the Imperial Roman Army. In all probability no such rule existed, it would undoubtedly have revolved around either individual or unit preference.

Bows and arrows, although the most obvious, were not the only pieces of archery equipment. A bracer is required to protect the left wrist (the bow being held in the left hand) from the bow string after release when the 'Mediterranean' release is employed (**fig 44 & colour plate 11**). Whilst a bracer is not required for the 'Mongolian' release a thumb stall or ring is required, for the right thumb. The thumb stall or ring fitted onto the right thumb and was used to draw and hold the bow string without cutting the thumb. Where the 'Mediterranean' release was employed, leather 'shooting tabs' to protect the archer's fingers from the bow string may have been employed, although there is no evidence to either support or refute this. The bow required a case and the arrows a quiver, both of

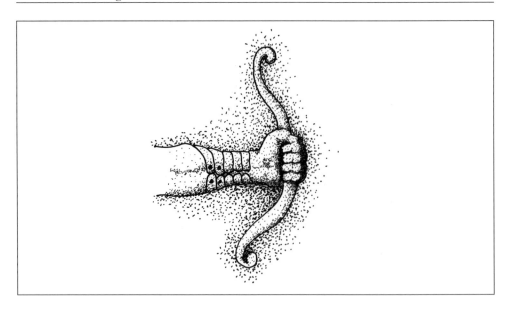

44   *An archer's bracer. A detail from Trajan's Column, Rome.*

(Drawn by K.R. Dixon)

which must be large enough to completely encase their respective contents, as both bow and arrows required protection from the damp. Out of all of these pieces of equipment there exists only one thumb stall in the archaeological record. No examples of thumb rings exist, and as for braces they are depicted on Trajan's Column, but again no examples survive.

Quivers appear on foot archers' gravestones, where they are depicted as being cylindrical in shape and worn diagonally across the soldier's back (**colour plate 11**). Unfortunately, we do not even possess this modest level of evidence for the foot archer's bow-case, as there are no representations or finds and we know nothing about them.

Foot archers were dressed, armed, and armoured as per a normal third-century infantryman, except that archery equipment was substituted for the shield, spear and javelins.

Evidence for the continued use of the sling in the third century comes from the finds of some stone shot (of possibly third century date) from Buciumi, Romania. However, there is no reason to doubt that lead slingshot was also used in this period. A mid- to late-second century sling pouch has tentatively been identified at Vindolanda, Great Britain (**fig 45**), made from thick cattle-hide and decorated with geometric patterning. If it were indeed a sling pouch then the difference between it and those used in the third century was probably negligble.

Having looked at the evidence for construction, the next things to consider are use, range and effectiveness. There are two methods of using a sling, either

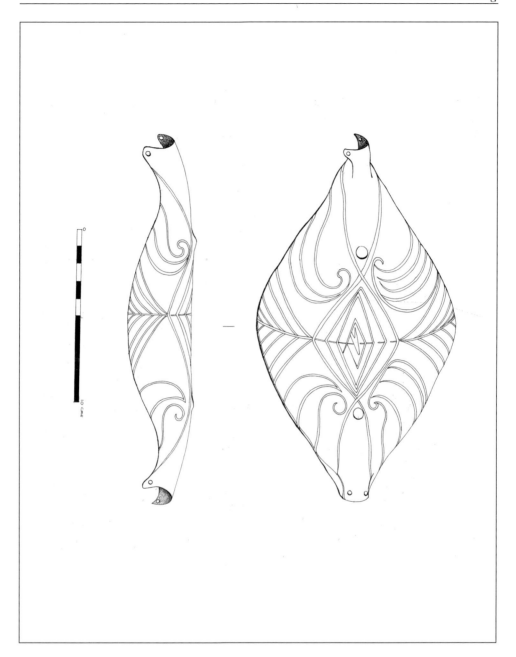

45   *The sling pouch from Vindolanda, Great Britain.*

(Redrawn by M. Daniels from Birley 1996)

swinging it by the side of the body or alternatively by swinging it above the head. In either case a great deal of skill and training was required to ensure that the shot carried in the correct direction every time, and, if the slinger was stationed behind his own infantry, that the arc of the cast was good enough to carry it safely over these friendly troops. Novice slingers could just as easily send the shot either straight up or backwards or not far enough in the correct direction. Thus training was a most definite prerequisite of sling use, and it appears from what little evidence there is that basic training with the sling was a universal requirement for the infantry arm of the Roman Army. Specialist units of slingers may have existed in the Roman Army of the third century, although, there is no evidence to either prove or refute this.

As with the bow no definite range can be placed on the sling, estimates range between 150-400m, with the lower end of this range being more probable under battlefield conditions.

The sling in the Ancient World was viewed as an effective weapon of war; indeed in the fourth century Vegetius (I.16) writes that it was 'more dangerous than any arrow'. This was because of its invisibility in flight and its concussive rather than penetrative effect. This concussive effect gave the slinger the ability to kill or incapacitate even armoured opponents. The shield was an effective defence against the sling shot, however its invisibility reduced the shield's effectiveness, and the soldier confronted by waves of such shot may well have succumbed, shield or no.

In terms of tactical deployment Trajan's Column places the slinger on the flanks of an army in battlefield formation, whereas Vegetius places them behind the infantry shieldwall. Whatever the case was in the third century we do not know, both deployments are practical and it most likely depended upon both battlefield circumstances and the individual prejudice of the commanding general.

16 Artillery

Our artillery was extraordinarily good and nothing could possibly live under its fire.

The Diaries of Lord Moyne, referring to the capture of Messines. 1917

The spear, sword, javelin and bow, are all weapons which were wielded by a single individual and which relied on bodily strength. Artillery was different; indeed, it was unlike any of the other weapons so far discussed, being a crew-served, mechanical construct, whose power was technologically derived. Bearing this in mind, it is therefore more appropriate to discuss use before type.

The term artillery conjures up a number of images; most immediately the great artillery bombardments of the Great War, 1914-1918, but also of Napoleon, both at the Siege of Toulon, 1793, and at the Battle of Waterloo, 1815. It does not, however, immediately conjure up the Ancient World, or if it does then the image is more one of sieges than of battles. Artillery on the battlefield is most definitely perceived as belonging to the age of gunpowder, namely from the Renaissance onwards. This picture is reinforced by the view that the Medieval period was one of cavalry charges and sieges, although in fact guns were used on the field of Crecy, 1346, by the English. In fact the Ancient and Medieval periods tend to be seen as having identical artillery use, if not weapons; and that use was most definitely siege warfare. The weapons of the battlefield were hand held and distance shooting was provided by contingents of archers.

In the main this view is correct, as artillery in antiquity was primarily deployed during sieges. The Roman Army, of course, employed artillery during sieges, no matter which side of the wall they were on. Using a combination of torsion, bolt- and stone-throwing machines in both defence and attack, the Romans were masters of siege warfare. In specific terms bolt-throwers in the main were used as anti-personnel weapons. In defence, Caesar's *African War* (29), describes an incident in 46BC when a bolt-firing artillery piece on the walls of Leptis was used to disperse a squadron of enemy cavalry. Whilst in attack, Tacitus (*Annals*, II.20) narrates an incident Germany, in AD15, where they were used by Germanicus to lay down a barrage of suppressing fire on a German rampart. Stone-throwers also had anti-personnel role, and Ammianus Marcellinus records their use in this capacity during the defence of Amida, AD 359 (XIX.8.7), and during the storming of Maiozamalcha, AD 363 (XXIV.4.16).

A further use of artillery during siege operations was in what would today be called counter-battery fire. The Germanic attitude to sieges is probably best typified by Fritigern's advice before the second unsuccessful Gothic assault on the city of Adrianople, in AD378, which was to hold yourself 'aloof from the miseries of a siege,' (Ammianus Marcellinus, XXXI.15.15). However, Rome did not always face such aloof opponents; the Greeks, Carthaginians, Sassanid Persians, and indeed other Romans all undertook siege operations and it was against these that counter-battery fire would have been employed. This would have taken two forms, but the desired end result was the same in both cases. In attack, the purpose of such shooting was to eliminate the enemy's artillery; in defence as well as destroying enemy artillery, such shooting was also used to destroy battering rams, siege towers and sheds. Bolt-throwers used large armour-piercing fire-bolts, which were designed to become trapped in the structure of the enemy engine and to set it on fire. Whereas stone-throwers simply relied on the weight of their missile to crush the target.

However, artillery also had a limited battlefield use, and although it was an uncommon feature of open warfare, it was still a feature and thus requires examination. The battlefield use of artillery, by the Roman Army, appears to have been confined to the bolt-throwing engine; stone-throwing engines do not appear to have been used.

Artillery has two main advantages over other weapon systems; firstly, it has the ability to kill at a great distance, far exceeding anything achievable with hand held weapons, and secondly, even at long range its missiles could still fatally penetrate both shield and armour. In the Modern Age, the age of gunpowder and cordite, shrapnel shells, high explosive shells and even bouncing solid shot (cannon balls), can cut huge swathes through advancing troops. The same cannot be said for torsion artillery, where a single bolt might be expect to pierce one or maybe two people at once (Ammianus Marcellinus, XIX.5.6). However, despite this apparent disparity of effect, ancient artillery could be just as devastating as modern artillery.

Artillery has two effects, the obvious physical effect and the equally destructive, but more insidious, morale effect. The effectiveness of torsion artillery on the ancient battlefield owed more to the latter than the former. The deployment of such weapons by the Romans, gave them the ability to inflict casualties on the enemy before the enemy were in a position to reply. This would have had a twofold morale effect. For those on the receiving end of such a bombardment, their morale would have dropped. They, the enemy, would be taking casualties, their armour would be useless and they would have no defence save retreat. They would also as yet be unable to reply, further depressing morale. For the Romans, however, this picture would be reversed. This ability to safely inflict casualties on the enemy, combined with the knowledge of the effect of these casualties, would only have served to increase Roman morale.

In terms of actual battlefield deployment, two methods were employed. The

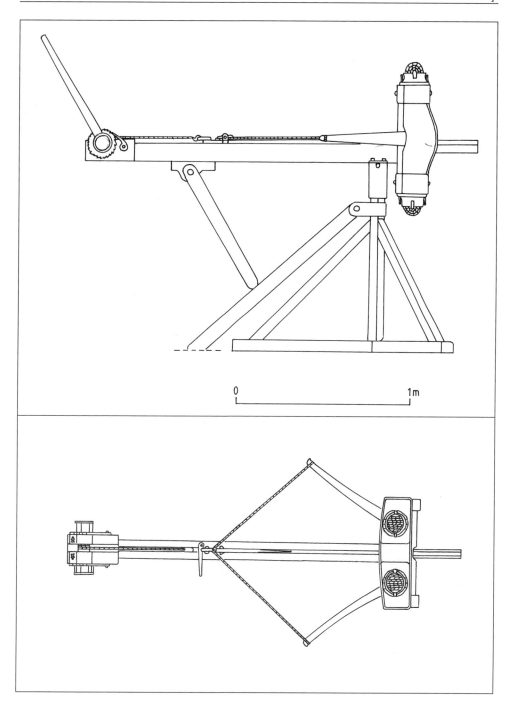

0   1m

46   The catapulta *of Vitruvius — plan and elevation.*

(Redrawn by K.R. Dixon from Baatz 1978)

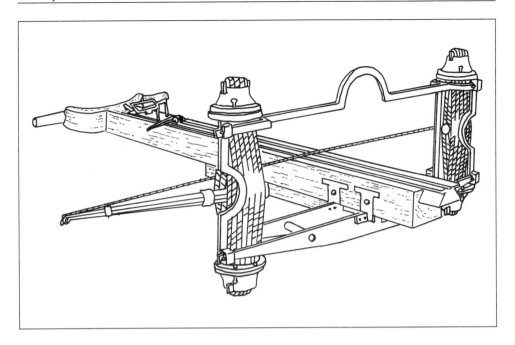

47   *The* cheiroballista.

(Redrawn by K.R. Dixon from Baatz 1978)

bolt throwers could be placed either on the flanks, or at the rear of the centre. Arrian, in his battle against the Alans, AD 135, (*Ektaxis kat' Alanon* 19), rested his flanks on high ground and placed his artillery on the flanks, behind a screen of infantry. Although we told that they fired over the heads of their own troops, our uncertain knowledge of both the geography and the exact troop dispositions, do not allow us to say whether the fire was direct or indirect. The deployment of artillery to the rear of the centre was depicted on Trajan's Column and advocated by Vegetius (II.15, III.14 and III.24). In the case of Trajan's Column, the artillery was placed on higher ground behind the main force, thus allowing the crew to engage in direct shooting. Vegetius' disposition, however, at the very rear of the main body of infantry, but in front of the reserve, only allows for indirect fire.

As for the actual artillery pieces themselves, there were as has already been stated two basic groups (bolt- and stone-throwers) in service with the Roman Army in the third century. These groups can be further broken down into four types, two per group. The *catapulta* and *cheiroballista*, were twin armed torsion bolt-throwers; the *ballista*, was a twin armed torsion stone-thrower; and, finally, the *onager* which was a single armed torsion stone-thrower.

The *catapulta* (**fig 46**) worked by placing two cord springs under tension. This was achieved by winding the springs around iron levers (one on each end of the spring, making four in total); once wound, they were held in place using metal washers. The springs were housed in a wooden frame, which was strengthened

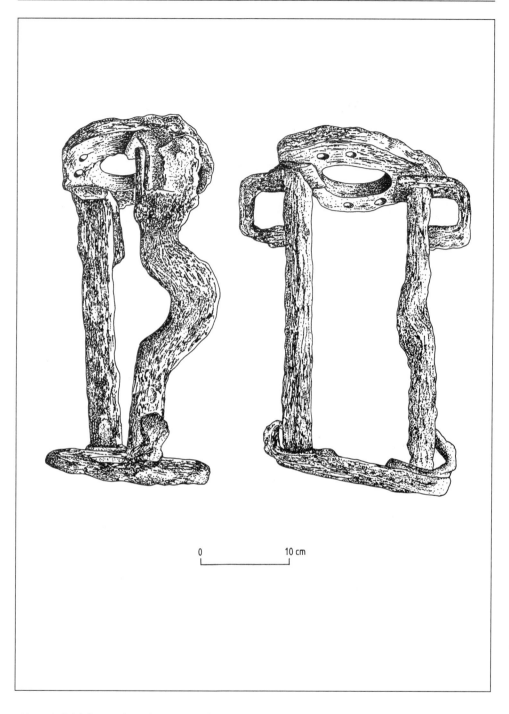

48   A field frame (kambestrion) *from Orsova, Romania.*

(Redrawn by K.R. Dixon from Gudea and Baatz 1974)

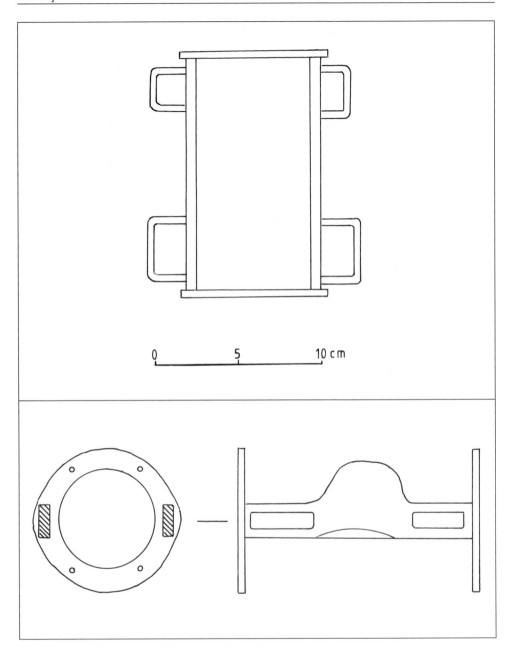

0   5   10 cm

49   *A field frame* (kambestrion) *from Gornea, Romania.*

    (Redrawn by K.R. Dixon from Gudea and Baatz 1974)

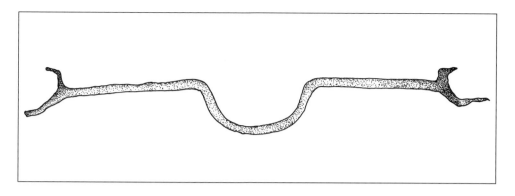

50   An arched strut (kamerion) *from Orsova, Romania.*

(Redrawn by K.R. Dixon from Gudea and Baatz 1974)

with metal corner plates. An arm was inserted into the centre of each spring, and the arms were then connected by a sinew bow string. Passing through the centre of the spring housing, at an angle of 90 degrees, was the case, which held the trigger mechanism. The centre of the string engaged the iron trigger mechanism. The trigger mechanism was attached to a freely moving slider which sat in a groove, which ran the length of the case. The slider was drawn back using a windlass, mounted on the end of the case. The drawing back of the slider, and thus the bow string and arms, by the windlass placed the springs under a greater degree of tension, and this provided the energy to shoot the bolt. Once the slider was fully drawn, the bolt was placed on the machine, final adjustments to the aim would occur, the trigger would then be released and the bolt shot. The whole thing was mounted on a stand, using a universal joint. As to its role, the *catapulta* was a siege engine, used in both attack and defence.

Despite its name, the *cheiroballista* (**fig 47**) was bolt-throwing, and was thus in effect a *catapulta*. In terms of the construction and mechanics of operation, the *cheiroballista* followed the same pattern as the *catapulta* with only two, possibly three, differences. Firstly, it was far smaller. Reconstructions have shown that the whole piece (minus stand) could have been carried by one man. Secondly, the spring housing was entirely metal. No third-century examples survive. However, fourth-century finds, from Romania, of field frames and an arched strut, exactly parallel the types used in the third century (**figs 48, 49 & 50**). Thirdly, the draw mechanism may have differed. The *cheiroballista* may have employed a winch, conversely it could have been drawn by hand. If hand drawn then the butt-end would have been curved, as the machine would have been cocked by first bracing the stomach against the butt, and then pulling back the string with both hands. As well as being used in siege operations, the *cheiroballista* was also used in open warfare, and it was this type of artillery piece which featured in the lines of battle described by both Arrian and Vegetius. When used in open warfare it was carried

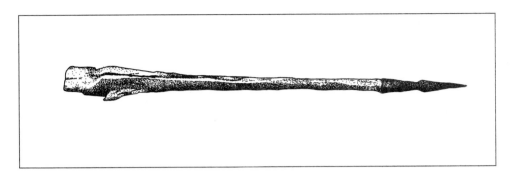

51   *A bolt from Dura Europos, Syria.*

(Drawn by K.R. Dixon)

on a two wheeled, mule drawn cart (*carroballista*, Vegetius III.14), and according to Trajan's Column, this cart could also act as a firing platform. However, these carts should not delude us into viewing the *cheiroballista* as horse artillery, they were field artillery pieces, used in fixed positions and did not gallop around the battlefield offering mobile fire support.

The *onager* (or wild ass), which was probably first introduced into the Roman Army in the third century, was a large, powerful, single, vertically armed, stone-throwing engine (Ammianus Marcellinus XXIII.4.4-7). It was in effect a torsion version, of the staff-sling; as the stone sat in a sling pouch on the end of the arm. It was only used during siege operations, and required a very firm base on which to stand (either turf or sundried bricks), as the shock waves produced by its use could, according to Ammianus (XIII.4.5), even shatter stone walls.

The second type of stone throwing artillery piece in use was the *ballista*. Construction was similar to that of the *catapulta*, save that it was larger and employed a band rather than a bow string. The remains, copper-alloy corner fittings, counter-plates, torsion washers and nailed sheeting to cover the front, of a third-century example found at Hatra, Iraq, had a frame 0.84m (2¾ft) high and 2.4m (8ft) long. The Hatra find was probably of medium calibre and larger pieces would have existed. The *ballista,* like the *onager,* was only used in siege warfare.

All of the above artillery would have been crewed by legionary personnel. Crew numbers would have varied depending upon the size of the artillery piece, but would not have been less than two men (the probable size of the crew of a *cheiroballista*).

Finds of the actual missiles themselves also occur. Rounded stones of various calibres have been found at both Dura Europos and at Buciumi, Romania. Iron *catapulta* bolt-heads are found throughout the Empire. The heads themselves are pyramidal in cross-section, as leaf-bladed heads would have proved too unstable in flight. The bodies of the bolts have also survived, with some 30 examples having been found at Dura Europos (**fig 51**). They were wooden, mainly ash, but also birch and pine, 34-37.5cm (13-14¾in) long, and tapered from approximately

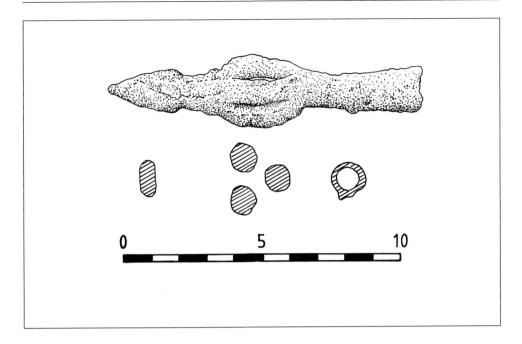

*52   The socketed head of fire-bolt from Dura Europos, Syria. Of note is the cage formed
       by the three curving bars.*

(Redrawn by K.R. Dixon from James 1983)

3cm at the rear to 1.4cm at a point 2cm below the tip (without the iron head). The
bolt-bodies had three maple wood vanes or flights, 5cm long, and the tail of bolt
started 4.5cm from the end and was shaped to fit the V slot on the trigger. The
head attached to the body by a small bronze pin.

   Also found at Dura Europos was the head of a fire-bolt (**fig 52**). The head was
11.3cm (4½ in) long, and had a small flat V-shaped blade. The blade attached to
the socket by three curved bars, which formed a cage. The cage would have held
the flammable material.

   Maximum effective range was according to Ammianus Marcellinus (XXIII.4.3)
further than the eye could see. This has been translated into approximately 400m,
although aimed, such shooting would have been inaccurate. Accurate aimed
shooting is believed to have been achievable at ranges of up to 185m.

17 Other equipment

The knapsack may be reduced to the smallest size possible.
but the soldier should always have it with him.

Napoleon, *Military Maxims*, LIX. 1831

Clothing

The third-century fashion on *stelae* for depicting the deceased unarmoured proves
a problem when it comes to the study of the armour of the period, but proves
opportune when we come to look at the clothing worn by the soldiers
(**colour plate 1**).

Fashion, as it is wont to do, changed. *De rigueur* for the Roman soldier from the
late second/early third century was the long sleeved, knee length tunic and long
trousers. The impetus for this change is unknown; Dio (LXXV.2.6) complained
that Septimius Severus filled Rome with soldiers 'most savage in appearance', and
indeed barbarianisation, in the form of greater recruitment from the fringes of the
Empire, may have played a large part in this change of style. Whatsoever may have
been the reason(s) behind this change, the reasons for its continuance are possibly
easier to understand, and are tied up with the idea of the Emperor as *commilito*
(fellow soldier).

One of the methods used by the Emperor to maintain the support of the Army
was to represent himself as a soldier, 'one of the lads' so to speak, a *commilito*. This
effect was achieved partly by sharing the soldiers' experiences on campaign; partly
by actually referring to the soldiers in speeches, conversations, letters and
documents as *commilitones* (fellow soldiers); and partly by dressing as a soldier. The
system then becomes rather self perpetuating. The Emperor dresses as a soldier in
order to help insure the support of the Army, the soldiers are wearing 'the new
fashion', the Emperor thus continues this fashion, with only minor alterations in
decoration and quality, so as not to alienate the Army.

As to the actual garments themselves, the representational evidence, from a
combination of *stelae*, Sassanian reliefs, and frescoes from Dura Europos, show
knee length, long sleeved tunics, which were quite tight at the wrists and where
colour survives, they are white. Decoration took the form of purple bands on the
hem and cuffs or as purple *clavus* bands running over both shoulders to the hem.

Both tight and loose fitting trousers, of a variety of colours, are depicted.

The artifactual evidence, particularly from Dura Europos, points to woollen tunics which were woven in one piece, decoration included, with a slit for the neck. As to the type of dye used for the decoration, madder based dyes tended to substitute for the more expensive true purple. The best parallel for the type of trousers worn comes from the third-century Thorsbjerg bog deposit, where a pair of woollen trousers with integral feet were found.

In two areas of dress there was a continuance of fashion from the second century. Third-century gravestones show the continued use of the *sagum* style of cloak by the Army. This was basically a rectangle of cloth, with either fringed hems or corner tassels, chocolate/reddish-brown in colour, which was worn fastened by a disc brooch on the right shoulder. This left the cloak open down the right-hand side. The other area of continuity was in the form of footwear employed, *caliga* been replaced in the second century by the hobnailed boot and this state of affairs continued into the third.

Belts

The belt in the third century retained its symbolic significance, in that the wearing of belts distinguished soldier from civilian. However, it changed its form; gone are the belts designs and aprons of the early Empire. The new fashion, depicted on gravestones and confirmed by the archaeology was for a broad waist-belt with a ring buckle.

Although no actual belts survive, and all that remains are the fittings, the representational evidence is clear enough to allow us to establish how this design of belt worked. The tapering belt ends passed through the ring buckle from the front, each end then folded back onto itself and was held in place by a single stud. In a number of cases the right hand end was extended and hung in a crescent before hanging down to the level of the right knee. This crescent could be above the belt, before hanging down either in front or behind the belt to knee level. Alternatively, it could hang below the level of the belt, in which case it would then loop over the belt, from either the front or back, before again hanging down to the level of the knee. The method chosen was probably one of individual preference, but in all cases the extended right hand end terminated in either one or two strap-ends (**colour plate 1**).

The buckles themselves were either copper-alloy or plain iron rings, with some of the copper-alloy examples having an extension which fastened over one of the studs (**fig 53**). Examples of the above exist both with and without a tongue. The studs themselves are very common and were fungiform in shape. Rectangular buckles, which operated on the same principle as the ring buckle, are also known. Existing examples incorporate an open work design in the centre; however, plain examples of this form occur on some gravestones, although, to date none have been found.

53   A ring buckle from Weissenburg.

(Redrawn by K.R. Dixon from Oldenstein 1976)

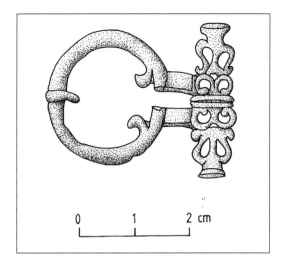

Strap-ends came in a wide variety of shapes and were attached either by riveting straight onto the leather or via metal hinges which were themselves riveted onto the end of the belt. Decorative copper-alloy appliqués, some with either enamel or *millefiori*, have been found throughout the Empire. They occur in a variety of shapes and correspond to the belt stiffeners which are apparent on a number of third-century gravestones.

A variation on this was to use appliqués in the form of letters to spell out a word or phrase on the belt, thus turning the belt into a good luck charm. This, however, seems to have been a regional fashion, limited in popularity to Danubian troops, although outlying examples occur at both Dura Europos and more famously at Lyon, France. The Lyon example, which has been dated to *c*.AD197, has cast separate letters which spell out the words FELIX VTERE (use with good luck). The 'X' and 'VT' were cast in such away as to form the buckle and counter-plate respectively (**colour plate 11**).

Marching Equipment

Although the impedimenta carried by the legionary on the march changed not at all in the third century its distribution did. Marching equipment now formed part of the auxiliarie's standard kit, and indeed this change was very much in line with the whole trend of the third century. Namely the disappearance of the differentiation between legionary and auxiliary units, in terms of equipment style.

Confirmation of continuance of design, in the archaeological record, comes from number of sites throughout the Empire, with the Kunzing, Germany, iron horde providing a number of fine examples of pieces of marching equipment, including pickaxes, bill-hooks and entrenching tools (**fig 54**). A flask, dated to the third century, from Buch, Germany, is similar to an Antonine period example found at Newstead, Scotland, and points to a continuance of design in terms of the basic items of campaign equipment from the second- to third-centuries.

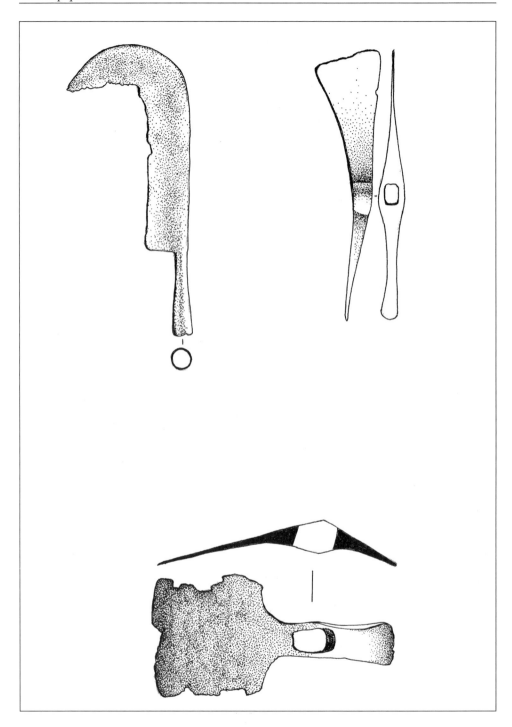

54   Marching equipment ; a pickaxe, a bill hook and an entrenching tool.

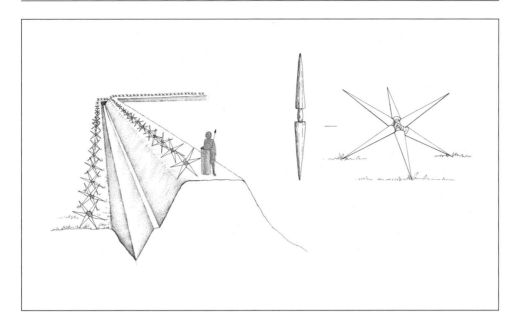

55   The palisade stake and its possible usage.

(Redrawn by M.Daniels from Gilliver 1993)

A potentially new addition to the marching kit of the period was the caltrop. Known from Hellenistic times they tend to be viewed as a piece of equipment used solely in the defence of fortifications, and indeed this was their primary function and they were used in this capacity during the third century AD. However, Herodian (IV.15.2-3) records their use in open battle stressing their success against cavalry, although it should be noted they would have been equally effective against infantry.

The 'palisade stake' continued to be used in the third century (**fig 55**). It retained its traditional role although it is now believed to have been used in a different manner. It was still used in the construction of temporary field fortifications, however, rather than having one end driven into the ground, it is now believed that they were tied together in groups of three to form large 'caltrops'.

On top of all of this the soldier would have also carried: bowls to eat from, a drinking vessel, a knife, a toilet set, gaming counters, dice, money, lucky charms, a bag to carry these things in and maybe writing materials. All the little day-to-day things which were as much a part of a soldier's life as his arms and armour.

Beneficiarii

The *beneficiarii, frumentarii* and *speculatores* were, in very general terms, soldiers engaged on special administrative duties, in effect junior staff posts. They were dressed and equipped the same as any other soldier of the period, be he legionary or auxiliary, with three exceptions. Their spears, belt and baldric fittings differed from the norm.

These spears, or rather spearheads, typified by examples from Kunzing and Wiesbaden, Germany (**fig 56**), are designed more with decoration and symbolism in mind than practical offensive use. This view is supported by other examples which have copper-alloy inlay silvering, slots, perforations and attached rings. They should therefore be seen more as indications of rank and position than as true spearheads. In pursuance of this function, and in order to facilitate ease of use, convenience being more important than other tactical considerations, the spearheads or 'benefiziarierlanze' were in all probability attached to shafts which were considerably shorter than those attached to the thrusting spears in use by the Army in this period. The staffs were thus more probably equivalent in height to those carried by *optiones* in the early Empire, and were almost certainly no higher than the height of the user.

The belt and baldric fittings all copy the design of the spearheads. In specific terms these fittings on the belt are in the form of strap-ends and decorative appliqués, where as on the baldric they act as *phalerae*. Although they all have a decorative function, their primary function was, as with the spears, to act as an indication of rank and position. Both as a reinforcement to the image projected by the spear and as a substitute if the spear was not being carried.

Command and Control

In equipment terms this was exercised on a personal level by the centurion's staff and at a unit level by the use of standards and musical instruments.

The evidence for the continued use of the centurion's staff is purely representational, as no actual examples survive. The *vitis* (vine stick) of earlier centuries was no longer employed, the new design was in many cases a longer, straight staff with a fungiform head. Despite this change of form its role, as symbol of office-come-swagger stick-come-implement of punishment, remained unaltered.

Vegetius (III.5) states that military signals were of three types: voiced, semi-voiced or mute. Voiced signals were shouted commands, semi-voiced were calls on instruments and mute signals were given using unit standards.

Writing in the fourth century Vegetius lists three types of musical instrument, the *tuba* (a straight trumpet), the *cornu* (a circular instrument) and the *bucina* (a silver bound auroch horn). In the third century evidence exists for the use of two out of these three instruments. A *cornu* is depicted on the mid-third-century Great

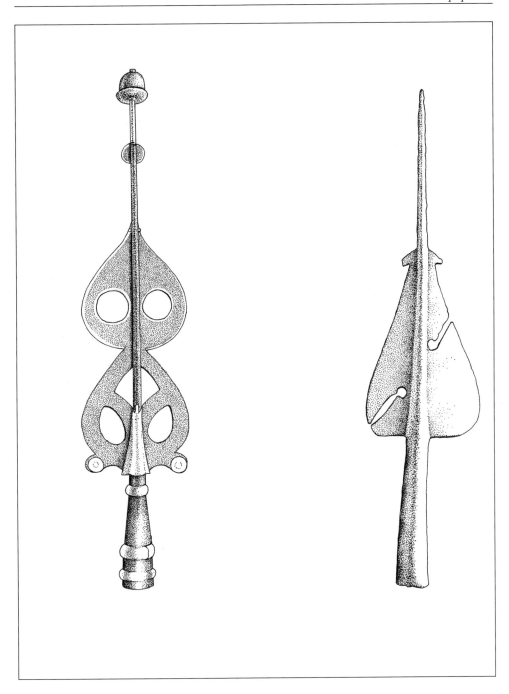

56 Benefiziarierlanzen. *The one on the left is from Wiesbaden, Germany, whilst the one on the right is from Kunzing, Germany.*

(Drawn by M. Daniels)

57   *A detail of the tombstone of Aurelius Surus, Istanbul.*

    (Drawn by M. Daniels)

58   The phalera *of Aurelius Cervianus.*

(Redrawn by K.R. Dixon from Casey 1991)

Ludovisi Battle Sarcophagus, Rome, and a *tuba* is depicted on the tombstone of
Aurelius Surus, Istanbul (**fig 57**). In battle these instruments were allegedly able
to produce five distinct sounds, which could order the Army to either, halt,
advance, pursue, withdraw or retreat.

The mute signals given by the standards appear to have been far simpler than
the voiced or semi-voiced variety. Standards were used by commanding officers
to mark the deployment locations of the various units under their command prior
to battle and to act as rallying points once battle had commenced. Soldiers were
literally expected to follow the standard.

As to the types of standard used both a bronze *phalera* (**fig 58**) dated to the third
century and the 'Tribune' fresco from Dura Europos depict *vexilla*. A *signum*
appears on the Great Ludovisi Battle Sarcophagus, whilst Vegetius (II.13 and III.5)
states that the *aquila* (eagle) was still carried. The *draco* (snake) was also used in the
third century, but was confined to the cavalry.

59 The vexillum *found in Egypt.*

(Drawn by M. Daniels)

As to the physical evidence, a *vexillum* was found in Egypt. It consists of a square of red linen, 0.47m high and 0.5m wide fringed along its lower edge. It was hung from a wooden or reed cross bar which had originally been attached to a spear. The decoration was painted and consisted of four gold angle-fillers (one in each corner), whilst in the centre the goddess Victory surmounts a globe and holds a palm branch in her left hand and a laurel leaf in her outstretched right hand. Unfortunately, this find is unprovenanced and may not date to the third century. However, leaving that to one side it remains the best evidence we have for the construction of the *vexillum*.

18 On strategy and tactics

Tactics teaches *the use of armed forces in the engagement*;
strategy, *the use of engagements for the object of the war*.

Carl von Clausewitz, *On War*. 1832

Strategic innovation

The third century tends to be viewed more as a period of strategic innovation than of tactical change, with debate centring on the strategic reforms of both Septimius Severus and Gallienus.

In the civil war that ensued following the assassination of Commodus, the Praetorian Guard backed the wrong man. As a consequence of which they were disbanded by Septimius Severus, and replaced by troops from the Emperor's own army, who were loyal to the new Emperor. In reforming the Guard, Septimius Severus probably (although the increase may be attributable to Commodus), doubled its size, from 8,000 to 15,000, and also increased the compliment of the Urban Cohorts. His reform of the Army, in terms of its size, did not stop there. He increased the size of the Army by raising new auxiliary units as well as three new legions *I, II,* and *III Parthicae*. Of the new legions *I* and *III Parthicae* were stationed in Mesopotamia, whilst *II Parthicae* was stationed at Alba, a mere twenty miles from Rome. This deployment, with the stationing of *II Parthicae* so close to Rome, gave Septimius Severus a force of 30,000 men in Central Italy. This force and the reasons behind its location have been much discussed, with debate centring on its role as both a strategic reserve and the nucleus of a field army (in the later Dominate style). However, both location and use militate against these interpretations.

Firstly, in terms of its location, Rome is patently not Milan, if it were then there would be no argument, but as it is not, then there is. In strategic terms, Rome was a backwater. Troops stationed at Rome would take far too long to reach any given flash point. Indeed their ability to speed to the scene would be no better than troops re-deployed from the Rhine or Danube. If the deployment of *II Parthicae* were as a mobile reserve, stationed within Italy, then the question must be asked why place them near Rome and not Milan? Which is a strategically important location, sitting as it does astride lines of communication which allow it access to Gaul and the Rhine, the Alpine passes and thus access into Germany, and also the Danube and the East.

The use of this force, certainly during the reign of Septimius Severus, also calls into question its function either as a strategic reserve or as the nucleus of a field army. For once established at Alba *II Parthicae* did not take the field under Severus, and was not present during his campaigns in the East or Britain. His successors, however, may have used either the whole, or a part of the legion, as a reserve; as it accompanied Caracalla to the East, was in Germany with Severus Alexander, and fought under Gallienus against the Alamanni. Subsequent use does not, however, prove initial intent and the purpose of *II Parthicae* may be divined more from the circumstances surrounding the accession of Septimius Severus, than from the use to which his successors put it.

In AD 193, Lucius Septimius Severus, the then governor of Pannonia Superior, was acclaimed emperor by the Danubian armies. Although he had to campaign in order to maintain his new found position (the civil war lasted until AD 197) Rome itself fell easily into his hands quite early on. This event undoubtedly proved crucial. The easy and for that matter early, fall of the Empire's capital, was in all probability what prompted an increase in the size of both the Praetorian Guard and Urban Cohorts, and also in determining the stationing of *II Parthicae* at Alba. As the location for a strategic reserve Rome was, as has already been stated, a backwater; however, in time of civil war Rome gained strategic importance, although this importance was psychological rather than military. What it was and what it represented were more important than its location. Being emperor in Rome gave the aspirant a far greater chance of being emperor everywhere. Septimius Severus undoubtedly understood this, he probably also realised that any failure on his part (be it perceived or actual) could well precipitate another civil war. Thus in order to, if not prevent civil war, at least help secure his throne against such an event, particularly when away on campaign, he created in effect a 'Garrison of Central Italy'. The 'Garrison', which would have consisted of *II Parthicae*, the Urban Cohorts, and that part of the Praetorian Guard not on campaign with the Emperor; would have acted as a field force of 20,000-30,000 men. The purpose of this force being to at least slow any usurper's passage to the capital, thereby giving Septimius Severus time to arrive with his army.

II Parthicae was thus in all probability created and located as a part of a strategic defence force rather than as a strategic reserve, and the only field army it may have been designed to form the nucleus of, was one destined to fight solely in Italy.

Returning to Milan, it was here in c. AD 259 that Gallienus (AD 253-268) stationed what has been seen by subsequent generations as the prototype for that later war winner — the cavalry army. Gallienus was, even by third-century standards, in an unenviable situation. Valerian, his father, had not only been defeated by the Persians, but also captured. Syria and the East were only saved by the intervention of the Roman protectorate of Palmyra. Although, in the process Odenathus, the king of Palmyra, made himself the virtual ruler of the East (Roman rule was re-established in c. AD 272 by the Emperor Aurelian). The situation in the West was, unfortunately for Gallienus, no better. The Western provinces had formed their own breakaway 'Gallic' Empire; and the Alamanni were massed in Switzerland. Gallienus therefore had little of the Empire left to rule and little recourse other than to campaign.

Initially formed in c. AD 255 to defend the Rhine frontier, it probably took the field with Gallienus, in AD 258 or 259, when he defeated the Alamanni, before finally being stationed at Milan. Milan, allegedly, being chosen as a base in order to counter the threat of invasion posed by the Gallic Empire (Zosimus I.40.1). Although we know little of the actual detail of its composition, its general structure can be postulated, and the reasons for its location and formation can be surmised.

The strategic location of Milan has already been discussed, and the presence or absence of the Gallic Empire in no way serves to alters the facts of the case. Gallienus need good lines of communication, Milan sat astride those lines. In logistical terms Milan is also well placed, it is surrounded by fertile land and the good communications facilitate the movement of supplies and provisions. The case for the strategic importance of Milan is further strengthened by its use as an Imperial residence in the fourth century.

Gallienus' cavalry army was doubtless formed from existing units, as he lacked the time to train new cavalry units from scratch. It also appears to have been made up of both whole units and vexillations (detachments on secondment from their parent unit). However, unlike previous similar concentrations (in terms of formation rather than composition) the force as a whole was described on coins as *equites* rather than *vexillatio*, or for that matter *ala*. Thus in terms of both its function and duration of existence it may well have been perceived at the time as being separate from both the provincial *alae* and from the vexillations of the early Empire.

The actual force itself was under the command of a single officer, and was made up of light, medium and heavy (?) cavalry as well as mounted infantry. Tribal contingents, the Mauri and Osrhoeni, armed respectively with javelins and bows, probably provided the light cavalry wing of the army. The medium to heavy cavalry contingents, armed with spear, sword and javelins, would have been drawn from vexillations of legionary cavalry, the *alae*, the *cohortes equitatae* and the *equites singulares Augusti*. Units of *contarii* and true heavy cavalry (*cataphractarii* and *clibanarii*), in whole or part, would also undoubtedly have formed part of the army's tactical make up. Mounted infantry detachments appear to have been formed from vexillations drawn from the Praetorian Guard, *II Parthicae* and the frontier legions.

The problems that Gallienus faced, and which resulted in the formation of the cavalry army, were both strategic and tactical. Strategically he was faced with both limited manpower and the possibility of either successive incursions on different fronts or a war on more than one front. Thus, rapidity of deployment was essential. Tactically, although infantry reigned supreme as 'queen of the battlefield', it had too slow a deployment time. Cavalry possessed the necessary speed, but lacked the infantry's tactical superiority. Although in the case of Roman cavalry this was to some extent mitigated by their training, as the Roman cavalryman underwent basic training to act as and was at times deployed as an infantryman (Caesar, *The Spanish War* 15; Frontinus, *Stratagems* II.iii.23; Tacitus, *Agricola* 37; Vegetius *Epitoma Rei Militaris* I.4; Procopius, *History of the Wars* I.xviii.43-49).

Gallienus would undoubtedly have had his mind firmly set on these problems, he needed a weapon/force that could move quickly and win battles. Thus, it is not surprising that he formed a combined cavalry/mounted infantry force and used that as his instrument. The inclusion of different types of cavalry (light, medium and heavy) gave him a broad tactical repertoire, and the ability to fight a part of the cavalry force dismounted gave him infantry. The inclusion of mounted vexillations (the Praetorians, *II Parthicae* and the frontier legions) allowed him to stiffen his dismounted cavalry with units of true infantry.

Whether or not Gallienus intended to found the first permanent mobile field force is both unknown and probably unknowable. He was in all probability more driven by necessity and expediency, than by any thoughts of creating a military renaissance.

Tactical change

Before the third century, unit designation determined troop type. The legions were close-order infantry whilst the auxilia were predominantly open-order infantry. The type of shield carried and the types of weapons employed by these units further reinforced this differentiation, although both were armoured. Therefore any categorisation of units in terms of heavy- and light-infantry, before the third century, should be seen more a reflection on their usage than on the levels of armour employed.

In the third century, this picture changes. There was now a marked lack of differentiation, in terms of equipment, between legionary and auxiliary units, with the more versatile auxiliary style of equipment being the preferred style for both types of unit. Coupled with this, the legions moved towards a situation where intra-unit tactical diversity was the order of the day, with the third century legion being made of a combination of close- and open-order infantry, archers, cavalry and artillery. Third-century auxiliary infantrymen maintained their ability to function as both open- and close-order infantry. Both types of unit were still highly armoured; indeed the level of personal armour generally increased in the third century, particularly for those troops who fought in close-order. This high level of armour provision, as will be seen, conferred distinct tactical advantages upon the Roman Army.

In broad terms the tactical picture of battlefield formation had not changed, the infantry still formed the centre and the flanks were either protected by cavalry, or pinned on secure terrain features. In specific terms the ideal order of battle is described by Vegetius, whilst an actuality is described by Dio. Vegetius' ideal, the Ancient Legion (which was in all probability a third-century AD infantry formation) was drawn up in six ranks (Vegetius II.15 and III.14). The first two ranks of which were close-order infantry, the third and fourth ranks were made up of archers and javelineers, the fifth was of catapults and slingers, whilst the sixth was a reserve of close-order infantry. Whilst Dio (LXXV) describing an actual engagement, states that the infantry were deployed in three lines. The first line was of close-order infantry, the second line was of javelineers and the third line of archers. The number of ranks per line is not stated and is therefore unknown. Although it is highly probable, that each line was at least three, possibly four ranks deep. Josephus and Vegetius both describe three/six rank deployment, whereas Arrian and Maurice favour a four/eight rank deployment. Infantry were therefore probably normally deployed in lines three or four ranks deep, although they may have been deployed in a deeper formation (six/eight ranks) when facing cavalry.

The order of events, for the infantry, in any battle of the period would be roughly as follows, firstly deployment, secondly a skirmish/missile exchange phase, and finally close-order infantry combat. The first phase has already been described; the second phase would have been initiated by the artillery, if deployed. Bodies of archers and javelineers drawn from Dio' second and third lines and Vegetius' middle ranks would have carried out the actual skirmishing itself. Against unarmoured western barbarians, the Roman's ability to field armoured skirmishers (armour should not be perceived as a bar to rapid movement) would have allowed them to dominate this phase of the battle. In the East, however, a greater degree of parity, in terms of armour provision, existed. In either case it was in the Romans best interest to prolong this phase, as their logistical superiority allowed them to expend a far greater quantity of missile (arrows, slingshot, bolts) than their enemies. At the conclusion of this phase, the skirmishers would have withdrawn and reformed behind the close-order infantry, whose job it now was to decide the issue.

For the infantryman of the third century, gone was the volley and charge of previous centuries, close-order combat now revolved around the line. Dio (LXXXV) merely describes the lines as closing to contact. Vegetius (III.20) on the other hand describes a number of different ways to attack in line, ranging from a general advance, to an oblique attack with one or other of the flanks refused, to an attack with the centre refused. Alternatively the line could hold its position and receive the enemy, or part of the line could form a wedge or column of attack and use that to destroy the enemy. Attacking in line is a slow process and it requires a great deal of training and discipline. The line must be kept dressed during any advance to prevent tears and gaps forming. A line that lacks complete cohesion and integrity will quickly and easily succumb to the enemy. At times, temporary field obstacles (pits and trenches) were dug, and caltrops scattered in order to precipitate the break up and thus the destruction of the enemy's line (Dio LXXXVI, Herodian IV.15.2-3).

Vegetius' wedge (III.19) was in all probability a trapezoidal column of attack. The column is far faster means of moving troops than the line, and a column of attack was the best way of quickly moving a body of infantry across the killing zone. It worked by using its speed and momentum to punch a hole in the enemy's front, which would then be exploited by the cavalry, who would in theory role up the enemy and thus rout them.

Howsoever the attack developed the front rank would have lowered their spears crouched behind their shields and prayed to their gods (**colour plates 12 & 13**). Whilst the rear ranks or lines would keep up a constant rain of missiles over the heads of their own side and into the enemy. Friendly fire casualties were inevitable. Thus, in the bloody carnage of the shieldwall, it is hardly surprising that the close-order infantryman was very heavily armoured. Nor is it surprising that the Roman infantryman's panoply reflected that of the Greek hoplites who first developed this the decisive infantry engagement.

Finally one side or another would break, tears and gaps would form and be exploited. Exploitation would, in theory, develop into collapse, which would hopefully develop into rout, with the defeated side suffering massive casualties. Here the Romans were lucky; the high levels of training, discipline and armour proved cumulative, and combined to make the Roman close-order infantryman harder to kill and thus made the line harder to break.

The Roman Army in the third century, as in previous centuries, was not endowed with any technological superiority, but as in previous centuries, it maintained a resource and organisational superiority which gave it a distinct tactical advantage over its enemies. As to the tactical changes, these changes should be seen for what they were; namely an adaptation in response to the prevailing conditions of the day. Change and the ability to respond and adapt should not be taken as signs of decline, they are in fact quite the opposite, and it should be remembered that the successful army changes over time, it does not stand still.

Appendix: Description of the colour plates

Plate 1: Unarmoured infantryman

This shows a typical third-century infantryman in undress uniform. He is wearing a white knee length, long sleeved tunic, which is cut tight at the wrists. The decoration on the tunic, which takes the form of purple bands on the hem and cuffs, is copied from wall paintings found at Dura Europos, Syria. The infantryman is wearing long, loose fitting woollen trousers with integral feet. On his feet, he wears hobnailed boots; the style illustrated is copied from an example found at Zwammerdam, Netherlands. The broad waist belt has the archetypal ring buckle, and the extended right hand end of the belt has the typical split and hinged straps-ends, which are a common feature of the period. The double phallus good luck charm is also ubiquitous, with examples occurring throughout the Empire. The soldiers cloak (*sagum*) has fringed hems and is fastened on the right shoulder with a disc brooch. Just showing above the level of the cloak is a scarf. The hairstyle, beard and moustache are copied from a bust of the Emperor Caracalla (AD 211-17).

Plate 2: *Thoracomachus*

Worn over the tunic, which would have been unbelted, the *thoracomachus* was the first stage in the soldiers arming process. No contemporary examples or illustrations survive, the reconstruction is thus based upon Anonymous' description in *De Rebus Bellicis,* and upon later Medieval manuscript illustrations and surviving Medieval examples of similar garments. The *thoracomachus*, as will be seen, conforms to the size of the infantryman's body armour; with the side splits facilitating ease of movement, and the collar helping to counteract the armour's friction. The infantryman's scarf is wrapped around his neck, acting as a cloth stock. The *pilleus* is worn as helmet padding.

Plate 3: Armoured infantryman   Mail 1

The second stage in the arming process required the infantryman to put his body armour on over the *thoracomachus*. Based upon an example found at Bertoldsheim, Germany, the soldier is wearing the knee length, long sleeved mail shirt that was the norm in this period. The actual shirt itself is made up of panels of iron mail, which are joined together by copper-alloy links. Tight neck closure is achieved using embossed copper-alloy breastplates.

Plate 4: Armoured infantryman   Scale 1

Alternatively a scale shirt could have been worn. The example illustrated is knee length, with side splits. The neck is edged with leather, as per the Carpow example, whilst the breastplates are copied from a set found at Manching, Germany. Linen *pteruges* are attached to the scale backing to provide a degree of protection to the vulnerable armpits. The shirt lacks integral sleeves.

Plate 5: Armoured infantryman   Mail 2

This next stage in arming sees the infantryman donning more armour, plus the first of his weapons. His lower legs are now protected by greaves, the examples illustrated are from Kunzing, Germany. Around his neck, protecting his throat is a scale gorget, copied from the Derveni find. Hanging by his right hand side he has a military dagger, the one shown is from Copthall Court. His *spatha* hangs from a plain baldric fitted with an eagle *phalera*. The sword has a plain bone or ivory hilt and is copied from one of the Nydam bog finds, the wooden scabbard is leather covered and has a box chape, the back of which is visible.

Plate 6: Armoured infantryman   Scale 2

Here the sleeves have been added to the scale shirt, they would have been attached by cloth ties. The actual scales on the sleeves are smaller than on the body in order to facilitate flexibility. The *pteruges* as well as protecting the armpits also help to protect the join between body and sleeves. In **Plate 5**, the mail is shown belted, and the belt does serve a practical purpose in that it helps to support the weight of the armour. The scale illustrated here is not belted and this is again for a practical reason. When scale is belted the smooth glancing surface is disrupted and the linen backing exposed, in order to prevent this dangerous reduction in the armour's protective capability scale was in all probability worn unbelted. The scabbard and baldric fittings on the *spatha* are copied from the Lyon burial, and instead of a military dagger the soldier has a short sword.

Plate 7: Armoured infantryman   Mail 3

For many infantrymen of the period this would constitute the final stage of the arming process (**Plate 9** details a possible further stage). The copper-alloy helmet is copied from an example found at Buch, Germany; note the 'T'-shaped face opening, peak and lack of crossed reinforcing bars. The shield is a flat oval constructed using the plywood technique and covered with linen, the edging is leather. The decoration of the shield takes the form of a *Dioscurus* with a horse and is copied from a third-century cheek-piece found at South Shields, Great Britain. The infantryman now has his primary weapon — a thrusting spear. The length of which has been shortened to fit the available illustrational space, as was the case on the tombstones of the period. The decoration on the spear shaft would have been painted and is copied from an illustration in the *Notitia Dignitatum*. He is also armed with two javelins.

Plate 8: Armoured infantryman   Scale 3

Instead of a helmet, this infantryman wears a scale coif, as with the sleeves small scales are used, this is in order to provide both flexibility and an effective glancing surface. The coif is similar to the helmet in that it also has a small face opening, but differs in that it acts as its own gorget. The shield, javelins and spear are the same as in **Plate 7**, although the decoration on the spear shaft is in this case taken from the early Byzantine Ravenna mosaics.

Plate 9: Armoured infantryman   Mail 4

A possible final stage in the arming process, for infantrymen equipped with mail, was the addition of a solid scale shirt. The scale shirt has leather edging and neck closure is provided by the use of breastplates. It would have been worn in order to provide the soldier with extra protection against arrows, javelins and spear thrusts. The decoration on the back of the shield is copied from the Amazon Shield, Dura Europos, Syria.

Plate 10: Libyan Hide

The infantryman was expected to operate underarms in wet weather, in order to do so he wore a tunic made of Libyan hide. The garment illustrated is conjecture as no examples survive and the only illustrations of the Libyan Hide come from Renaissance copies of ninth- and tenth- century Carolingian manuscripts. The garment shown in the reconstruction is a simple leather tunic worn over both armour and *thoracomachus*, the seams are on the outside in order to reduce strain on the stitching (as was the case with seventeenth-century buff-coats). The garment could also possibly double as a groundsheet for soldier to sleep on.

Plate 11: Foot Archer

This figure is wearing a conical, copper-alloy helmet; the example illustrated is from Intercisa, Hungary, it is fitted with a mail curtain, which acts in place of cheek-pieces, neck guard and gorget. The body armour consists of a knee length, elbow length mail shirt, worn over a *thoracomachus*. The solid scale shirt provides an extra layer of protection. His secondary weapons consist of a military dagger (from Copthall Court) hung from a waist belt that bears the motto FELIX VTERE (from the Lyon burial) and a *spatha*. The *spatha* illustrated is the Khisfine, Syria, example, whilst the baldric is from Vimose, Denmark. His primary weapon is the composite bow, and the leather bracer on his left arm shows that he employs the Mediterranean method of release. The stiff leather quiver hangs by his waist in order to allow him to easily remove the arrows, the arrow spacer on the quiver is extrapolated from later medieval examples. The arrow he is holding has a bodkin (armour piercing) head.

Plate 12: Fighting stance as seen from the front

The infantryman would fight standing in a slight crouch, with his left leg forward, holding the spear underarm, so very little of the body is actually visible. The helmet covers most of the head, only the small 'T'-shaped face opening is exposed. The shield covers the body, the left arm, most of the right arm and the legs down to the knees, the lower legs are protected by the greaves and the right leg is obscured by the left leg.

Plate 13: Fighting stance as seen from the side

Here we have a better view of the fighting stance, the legs are bent and apart, and the back is straight (this stance would have been adopted no matter which weapon he was holding). The javelins are gripped behind the shield and both they, the sword and the military dagger are easily accessible. Unlike in **Plates 7-9** the spear is shown to the correct length.

Plate 14 and Cover: A reconstruction of the Heddernheim helmet

These plates show the new style of helmet worn by the third-century Roman infantryman. The bowl is iron, although the decoration is in copper-alloy, as is the peak and crossed reinforcing bars. The reconstruction is by H. Russell Robinson and is housed in the Museum of Antiquities, at the University of Newcastle upon Tyne.

Plate 15: A reconstruction of a dolphin scabbard-slide from Corbridge, Great Britain

This is a plan view of a reconstruction of a cast copper-alloy dolphin scabbard-slide found at Corbridge. The original is incomplete and measures 14.05cm long, with a maximum width of 1.8cm.

Plate 16: A reconstruction of the Carlisle eagle *phalera*

The centre of the *phalera* contains an eagle holding thunderbolts. The encircling inscription (which starts just above the eagle's head) reads OPTIME MAXIME CON[SERVA]; which translates as 'Best [and] greatest [referring to Jupiter] protect'.

Plates 17 and 18: A reconstruction of a box chape from Corbridge – front and back

These plates show a reconstruction of a copper-alloy box chape found at Corbridge, Great Britain. Like all box chapes it is flat-ended and has the typical trapezoidal profile common to this form. The front is decorated by a pair of crescentic perforations. The chape is glued to a wooden plug which projects from the bottom of the scabbard.

Plates 19 and 20: A reconstruction of a leaf-bladed spearhead and a butt-spike

These two objects together with 7-9ft of ash shaft formed the infantryman's primary weapon. The butt-spike was in effect a second spearhead, being used only after the spearhead had been lost.

Plate 21: Reconstructed leaf-bladed javelin heads

This plate illustrates quite the commonest form of javelin used by the army. The weapons here are similar to those depicted on the tombstone of Aurelius Mucianus.

Plate 22: A reconstruction showing the tail end of an arrow

The design of the nock and the position of the fletching show that this arrow was designed to be used by an archer employing the Mediterranean release.

Bibliography

Primary Sources

AMMIANUS MARCELLINUS

AENEAS *On the Defence of Fortified Places*

ANONYMOUS *De Rebus Bellicis*

ARRIAN *Ektaxis kat'Alanon*

CAESAR *The African War*

CAESAR *The Gallic War*

CAESAR *The Spanish War*

DIO *Roman History*

DIODORUS SICULUS *Universal History*

FRONTINUS *Stratagems*

HERODIAN

HOMER *Iliad*

JOSEPHUS *Jewish War*

JULIUS AFRICANUS *Kestoi*

MAURICE *Strategikon*

NOTITIA DIGNITATUM

POLYBIUS *The Histories*

PROCOPIUS *History of the Wars*

SCRIPTORES HISTORIAE AUGUSTAE

TACITUS *Agricola*

TACITUS *Annals*

TACITUS *Histories*

VEGETIUS *Epitoma Rei Militaris*

ZOSIMUS *New History*

Secondary Sources

The list of books and journals (given below) is by no means a comprehensive list of the secondary sources used in the writing of this book, nor for that matter is it intended to be so. It is more in the way of an introduction to the literature used, and should be seen as a guide to further reading. More complete bibliographies are provided on the equipment by Bishop & Coulston, 1993, *Roman Military Equipment*; and on the history and organisation, by Southern and Dixon, 1996, *The Late Roman Army*.

Books

Bishop, M.C. and Coulston, J.C.N. 1993: *Roman Military Equipment: from the Punic Wars to the fall of Rome*, London.

Campbell, J.B. 1984: *The Emperor and the Roman Army 31BC-AD235*, Oxford.

Connolly, P. 1981: *Greece and Rome at War*, London.

Dixon, K.R. and Southern, P. 1992: *The Roman cavalry: From the First to the Third Century AD*, London.

Edge, D. and Paddock, J.M. 1988: *Arms & Armour of the Medieval Knight*, London.

Elton, H. 1996: *Warfare in Roman Europe AD 350-425*, Oxford.

Ferrill, A. 1983: *The Fall of the Roman Empire: the Military Explanation*, London.

Griffith, P. 1990: *Forward into Battle: fighting Tactics from Waterloo to the Near Future*, Swindon.

Goldsworthy, A.K. 1996: *The Roman Army at War 100BC-AD200*, Oxford.

Hackett, General Sir J. (ed.) 1989: *Warfare in the Ancient World*, London.

Hanson, V.D. 1989: *The Western Way of War: Infantry Battle in Classical Greece*, New York.

Hanson, V.D. (ed.) 1991: *Hoplites: The Classical Greek Battle Experience*, London.

Keegan, J. 1978: *The Face of Battle*, Harmondsworth.

Knight, I. 1995: *The Anatomy of the Zulu Army: from Shaka to Cetshwayo 1818-1879*, London.

Lloyd, A.B. (ed.) 1996: *Battle in Antiquity*, London.

Randsborg, K. 1995: *Hjortspring: Warfare and Sacrifice in Early Europe*, Aarhus.

Rankov, B. 1994: *The Praetorian Guard*, London.

Robinson, H.R. 1967: *Oriental Armour*, London.

Robinson, H.R. 1975: *The Armour of Imperial Rome*, London.

Southern, P. and Dixon, K.R. 1996: *The Late Roman Army*, London.

Journals

Arma: Newsletter of the Roman Military Equipment Conference.
Available from M.C. Bishop, Braemar, Kirkgate, Chirnside, Duns, TD11 3XL.

The Arbeia Journal.
Available from The Secretary, The Arbeia Society, Arbeia Roman Fort, South Shields, Tyne & Wear, NE33 2BB.

Journal of Roman Military Equipment Studies.
Available from Oxbow Books, Park End Place, Oxford, OX1 1HN.

Index

Complied by S. Stephenson